Early German Music in Philadelphia

AMS PRESS

NEW YORK

Early German Music in Philadelphia

Robert Rutherford Drummond, Ph. D.

Sometime Harrison Fellow in Germanics at the University of Pennsylvania; Instructor in German at the University of Maine

UNIVERSITY OF PENNSYLVANIA

D. APPLETON & COMPANY
PUBLISHING AGENTS
NEW YORK
1910

Library of Congress Cataloging in Publication Data

Drummond, Robert Rutherford.
    Early German music in Philadelphia.

    Reprint of the 1910 ed., issued in series: Americana
Germanica. New series.
    Includes bibliographical references.
    1. Music--Pennsylvania--Philadelphia. 2. Music,
German. I. Title. II. Series: Americana Germanica.
Reprints.
ML200.8.P5D8   1972   781.7'43   72-1596
ISBN 0-404-09917-3

Reprinted from the edition of 1910, New York
First AMS edition published in 1972
Manufactured in the United States of America

International Standard Book Number: 0-404-09917-3

AMS PRESS INC.
NEW YORK, N. Y.   10003

TO MY PARENTS

FOREWORD

In this book I have sought to give a glimpse of the musical life of Philadelphia during the 18th Century, laying especial stress on the secular music, and considering principally the German music produced and performed, and emphasizing the high standard of musical taste at this time.

While confining myself to secular music, I thought it necessary in the first period to treat somewhat in detail the religious music, especially as the religious music was of more importance in the first half century than the secular music. So, too, I have gone into detail somewhat more in the first two periods than in the last, because these periods have not been so thoroughly investigated as the last period has. It may be objected by some, that I have not adequately considered the concert life of the last period. To these I would say that this period has been fully covered by O. G. Sonneck in his "Early Concert Life" in such a manner that I, at least, could not improve upon it.

It is hoped that this book may help to correct the false impression, that musical taste in America in the 18th century was an unknown quantity.

―――――

This study was undertaken at the suggestion of Prof. Marion D. Learned and to him I am especially grateful for aid and encouragement in preparing the work. To O. G. Sonneck of the Library of Congress I am greatly indebted not only for material found in his books on early American music, but also for his extreme kindness in placing at my disposal unpublished material. His suggestions and encouragement have been of great help to me. I wish to acknowledge here the courtesy extended to me by the officers and attendants of the Pennsylvania Historical Society and the Library of University of Pennsylvania and also the aid given to me by various friends.

This Study was submitted in partial Fulfillment of the Requirements for the Degree of Doctor of Philosophy, at the University of Pennsylvania, 1909.

ROBERT R. DRUMMOND.

Bangor, Me. Sept. 1, 1909.

TABLE OF CONTENTS.

INTRODUCTION.

The early immigration of Germans to Philadelphia increased to such an extent, that before the middle of the eighteenth century the English colonists became alarmed for fear that Pennsylvania might be alienated from the English crown, and be dominated by the German immigrants. Indeed, throughout the eighteenth century the greater part of the German immigrants landed at Philadelphia, and from there were distributed into other States. We should naturally expect, with so great a population of Germans in Philadelphia and the surrounding country, that these people would continually extend their influence, and constantly spread abroad their ideas of art, religion, music and literature.

Let us consider for a moment the condition of the Germans who landed in this country. In 1683, moved by William Penn's alluring proclamations of the glorious new world, as well as by the fact that freedom of conscience was granted in Pennsylvania to all, a band of German immigrants arrived in Philadelphia and founded Germantown. With the exception of the scholar, Francis Daniel Pastorious, there were no highly cultured men or women among them. These people were of the middle class, and were more interested in weaving and agriculture and religious salvation, than in the cultivation of the fine arts. The conditions in Germany were not conducive to culture.

The country was just recovering from the Thirty Years' War, and the strength of the people was being expended in building up the homes, and improving the land made desolate during that fierce struggle. At this time, too, the German people had little liberty, but rather were under the thumb of absolutism, which was at that time the great force in European countries. It was not an epoch favorable to the cultivation of the fine arts. There was no great literature, no great art, no great music. There was, however, a strong religious spirit, which is often the result of hardship and suffering. It is in the field of religion, too, that we find the best music during the seventeenth century, although it was not original in style, but simply a continuation of Luther's music.[1] The hymn writers of that time, both Catholic and Protestant, are not to be despised, and we need mention but a few, whose songs have lived even to the present day: as Paul Fleming (1609-1640) and Paul Gerhardt (1606-1676), Protestant; Friedrich Spee (1591-1635) and Johann Scheffer (1624-1677), Catholics. It can be said, then, with some degree of surety, that the performance of music by the early German settlers in Philadelphia was confined, in the province of music, to hymns.

In this department the Germans hold an important position; not only was their church music an essential part of their services, but the number of hymn-writers and the many editions of German hymn books published in Philadelphia testify to the love which these new settlers had for church music.

It is only necessary to mention a few of these hymn-writers to recall to mind the extreme productiveness of this style of literature and music. Among the most important hymn-writers were F. D. Pastorius, of Germantown; Johann Kelpius, of the Wissahickon; Conrad Beissel, of Ephrata, and Count von Zinzendorf, the Moravian.[2]

---

[1] Louis Elson, *National Music in America*, p. 18.

[2] Cf. for further information on this subject: J. H. Dubbs, *Early German Hymnology of Pennsylvania*; Hausmann, *German American Hymnology* 1683-1800, in *Americana Germanica* 1898, Vol. II. No. 3, p. II.

PART I

Beginnings before 1750

CHAPTER I.

Hymn Music of Germans in Philadelphia.

To Francis Daniel Pastorious has been assigned the honor of
being the first German hymn writer on American soil. Pastorious[1]
was born Sept. 26, 1651 at Sommerhausen, Germany, of cultured
parents of some means and position in society. His father Melchior
Pastorious had studied Catholic theology and also jurisprudence,
but had finally renounced his faith and had become a Protestant.
Needless to say Francis Daniel's education was not neglected. He
was sent to school in various places: as Windsheim, Basel, Nuremberg,
Erfurt, Strassburg where he studied law and the French language,
Jena where besides law he studied Italian, and finally he took his
degree of Doctor of Laws at Altdorf, 1676.

He settled now at Frankfurt am-Main and practiced his profession. He probably continued in this work until 1680, when, as
the companion of Johann Bonaventura von Rodeck, he made a
journey, extending over two years, through Holland, England,
France, Switzerland, and Germany. Upon his return to Frankfurt,
November, 1682, he became interested in the mysticism of Spener and
his companions, and the movement to America which they were
promoting—filled him with an ardent longing to share in it. So,
with the consent of his father who provided him with money, Francis
Daniel set sail for America and arrived in Philadelphia Aug. 20,
1683, six weeks before the other immigrants landed.

Pastorious was the only highly educated man in this colony. He
was looked up to by the other colonists for this reason, and also

---

[1]Hausmann, *"German American Hymnology* 1683-1800," in *Americana
Germanica* (hereafter. Am. Ger.) 1898, Vol. II, No. 3, p. ii.

because he was the agent of a land company formed in Germany for the purchase and sale of land in Pennsylvania. The new colonists chose as the spot for their new homesteads a tract of land not far from Philadelphia, where they founded Germanopolis or Germantown.

On Nov. 26, 1688, Pastorious married Ennecke Klostermanns and had two sons, whose descendants live at the present day. In 1691, Pastorious was elected to the newly-created office of "Bürgermeister," an office to which he was chosen three other times. Besides this office, he was for many years elected to the position of "Stadtschreiber," and was also schoolmaster at different times. He was known as a writer of some talent, and composed poems, hymns, epigrams, etc., in Greek, Latin, German, French, Dutch, English and Italian. I will close this bare outline with Pastorious' account of himself as quoted by Seidensticker:

"Der Verfasser dieses Manuscripts hat ein melancholisch-cholerisches Temperament und ist daher, nach Culpepper, sanftmüthig, zu einem nüchternen eingezogenen Leben disponirt, wissbegierig, unentschlossen, bescheiden, schüchtern, bedächtig, standhaft, und zuverlässig in seinen Handlungen, langsamen Witzes, vergesslich. Geschieht ihm Unrecht, so trägt er es nicht nach."

This remarkable man died Sept. 27, 1719.[2]

Pastorious' hymns are up to the standard of most hymns written at that time.

In point of time the next hymn writers were the so-called "Hermits of Wissahickon," a band of men and women steeped in German mysticism, and having a belief that the end of the world was soon to come and that their one love should be the Lord Jesus Christ; so on this account renouncing marriage as sinful. It was in this wilderness, beside the Wissahickon Stream about eight miles from Philadelphia, that this band of Pietists in the year 1694 took up

---

[2]The material for this sketch was obtained in great part from Seidensticker's, *Geschichtsblaetter (Bilder aus der Deutsch-Pennsylvanischen Geschichte)* pp. 34 ff. Also M. D. Learned. Life of Francis Daniel Pastorious.

their abode, and from whence issued the strains of hymns, reminding one, in some instances of love songs rather than praises to God.[3] There were in this congregation a number of men of high culture and lofty aims such as Johann Kelpius, Henry Bernhard Köster, Johann Gottfried Seelig, etc.

The most important man was Johann Kelpius, their leader, who composed the greater number of their hymns.[4] Kelpuis was the son of a pastor in Denndorf in the Siebenbürgian district of Germany. He studied theology at Altorf, where he was a pupil and favorite of the learned doctor, Johann Fabricius.

"Fabricius vertrat," says Seidenscticker, "die sogenannte irensche oder friedliebende Schule der Theologie, die von der bittern Fehde gegen andere Confessionen absah. Kelpuis, anfangs ein sternger Calvinist, griff den Gedanken an ein innerliches Christenthum begierig auf und bildete ihn unter andern Einflüssen weiter."[5]

In 1689, Kelpius obtained his master's degree. In the years following he composed an essay entitled: "Scylla Theologiae, aliquot exemplis Patrum et Doctorum, etc." About this time he must have obtained a knowledge of the religion of the mystics, and must also have come under the influence of Jacob Böhme's philosophy, and Spener's theosophy.

Such was the man who led the band of hermits, which arrived in Philadelphia, June 23, 1694. His life on the Wissahickon was

---

[3]Cf. Seidensticker. *Geschichtsblaetter*, p. 87 ff.
[4]S. Pennypacker. *Hymn Book of the Hermits of the Wissahickon* (*Penn. Mag. of History* Vol. XXV, p. 338.)
[5]Seidensticker. *Geschichtsblaetter* p. 91.

one of pious contemplation, and striving to follow out his idea of Christianity. He died 1708.[6]

The Hon. S. W. Pennypacker has in his possession a hymn book composed by these people, in which some of the hymns are dated 1707. He reports that Kelpuis wrote nineteen hymns; another writer possibly Köster thirteen hymns; and Seelig four hymns.[7]

Not only did these "Hermits" worship God with song, but they undoubtedly accompanied their voices with musical instruments, since we know that they brought the latter with them from London.[8] Also we find Kelpuis in one of his letters desiring that two clavichords with additional strings might be sent.[9] This simply goes to show that this little band of religious fanatics was not deficient in musical ability, and also that they carefully nurtured their love for music. Gradually these Pietists died or renounced their faith and were received into other religious societies,[10] and in the latter case one may be sure that their musical instruments went with them and were played and listened to with pleasure in a far wider circle than formerly.

It is not our purpose to consider in detail the various German hymn-writers in Pennsylvania, as the field is far too large, and besides the composers for the most part, were not inhabitants of Philadelphia. There are a few men, however, of sufficient importance to be considered, even though they lie somewhat without our field of operation. Perhaps the most picturesque figure in the history of American music in this century is Conrad Beissel of Ephrata Cloister. He not only evolved a *new* system of music, but was also the *first* composer of music in America. He wrote hymns and chorals in four, five, six, and seven parts, while usually in other congregations the hymns were sung in unison.[11]

The first edition of Ephrata hymns was published by Benjamin Franklin, Philadelphia, 1730, while different editions of new hymns

---

[6]For this sketch cf. Seidensticker. *Geschichtsblaetter*, pp. 91-100.

[7]*Penn. Mag. of History*, Vol. XXV p. 338.

[8]Cf. Seidensticker, *Geschichtsblaetter*, p. 89.

[9]Cf. Seidensticker, *Geschichtsblatter*, p. 100.

[10]Seidensticker, *Geschichtsblaetter*, p. 102.

[11]T. H. Sachse, *Music of the Ephrata Cloister*, p. 29 [hereafter, "*Sachse*."]

appeared in 1732, 1736, 1739, 1754, 1755, 1756 (2 eds.), 1762, and 1766.[12] Of these hymns, over 1,000 are attributed to Conrad Beissel. Not only did he compose music, but he also wrote the first treatise on harmony in America.[13] Concerning the quality of the music Dr. J. H. Sachse says: "The peculiar sweetness and weird beauty of the songs of the sisterhood, and the impressive cadence of the chorals and hymns of the combined chorus"[14] is strikingly seen.

Before the end of the century nearly all the sects of the Pennsylvania Germans had their editions of hymn-books, for the most part abridgements of those in use in the mother country. A few sects, however, had men versed in poetry as well as religion, and these helped to swell the hymn-books, already in use, with new songs. The Moravians were especially prolific, and under the direction of Count Nikolaus von Zinzendorf, who himself wrote over 130 hymns in this country, produced a work of some importance. "No authorized hymn-book for the Moravian church was issued in America during the colonial period, but a small collection printed at Germantown by [C.] Sauer [in] 1742, 'Hirtenlieder von Bethlehem' " was popular.[16] Zinzendorf was not the only hymn writer among the Moravians, since there were also his two wives, his son, Bishop Spangenberg and others, who had some ability in this line. In speaking of the "German-American Hymnology," Haussmann remarks that the hymns of all sects were subjective, excepting those of the Moravians.[17]

In the 18th century, Philadelphia and Germantown were the two—for a time the only two—important printing centres of Pennsylvania, and here it was that the greater number of German hymn books were printed. There can be no doubt, I think, that many of these German hymns were known to most of the inhabitants of

---

[12]*Amer. Ger.* Vol. II, No. 3, p. 19.   Dubbs, p. 9.

[13]Sachse, p. 22.

[14]Sachse, p. 29. (For further information on this subject consult the works quoted above.)

[16]Dubbs, p. 18 ff.

[17]*Am. Ger.* Vol. II, No. 3, p. 39.

Philadelphia, but as to whether or not these hymns had any influence upon the people, we are as yet, not prepared to say. At this time, we can do no more than enumerate the different editions of German hymn-books printed in Philadelphia and vicinity during the 18th century, although we hope that we may later investigate them thoroughly. In 1744 the Brotherhood of the Inspired produced an abridgement of a larger European collection. This became a favorite with the different Separatist bodies. It was called "Das Kleine Davidische Psalterspiel der Kinder Zions."[18] This book contains 530 pages, and was printed by C. Sauer, Germantown. In 1752 Sauer reprinted the "Marburg Reformed Hymn Book; 1753[19] "Die Kleine Harfe,"[20] 1762, Marburg edition of the Lutheran hymn-book,[21] and also in this same year the first edition of Schwenkfelder hymns,[21a] some of which were composed in this country, others taken from the Lutheran and Reformed hymn-books, but based, in great part upon the hymn-book of the Bohemian Bretheren. It contains 917 hymns.[22] In 1763 was printed the "Marburg Reformed Hymn-Book;"[23] in 1786 the earliest original collection of Lutheran hymns in this country, entitled "Erbauliche Liedersammlung;" 1788 "Liebliche und Erbauliche Lieder," "Unparteysche Lieder Sammlung," and others published by the German Baptist Society;[24] 1797 "Neues und vesbessertes Gesangbuch" printed by Steiner & Kammerer, Phila., 1799, a third edition of the Marburg Lutheran Hymn Book".[25] The total number of editions of German hymn-books during this century was twenty-two, but besides that there was a German hymn-book translated into English in 1795.

---

[18]Dubbs, p. 21.
[19]Dubbs, p. 25.
[20]Dubbs, p. 21.
[21]Dubbs, p. 21.
[21a]A. A. Seipt.   "Schwenkfelder Hymnology" (*Americana Germanica* vol. 7.)
[22]Dubbs, p. 16.
[23]Dubbs, p. 25.
[24]Dubbs, p. 21.
[25]Dubbs, p. 25.

CHAPTER II.

CHURCH MUSIC AND THE MANNER OF ITS PERFORMANCE.

It has already been mentioned that there were many German hymn-writers in Philadelphia in the early eighteenth century, and it is now in place to consider what was the quality of the music in the German churches at that period, and whether musical instruments of any kind were used in the Philadelphia churches.

For the first record it is necessary to go a little beyond Philadelphia to the Hermits of the Wissahickon. To this people undoubtedly belongs the honor of first using instrumental music in religious services. Of their voyage across the Atlantic, Kelpius says:

"We had also prayer meetings and sang hymns of praise and joy, several of us accompanying on instruments that we had brought from London."[26]

Evidently the instruments which they brought with them were not satisfactory or were regarded as inadequate for the worship of God, as Kelpius in a letter to friends in London asked that two clavichords with additional strings might be sent.[27]

Again the Hermits at the consecration of the new Swedish church—Gloria Dei—July 2, 1700, act as choristers and furnish instrumental music.[28]

The first German minister ordained in this country was Justus Falckner, who was consecrated by the Swedish Lutherans. In a letter to Rev. Heinrich Muhlen, of Holstein (1701), Falckner shows that, even at that early day, music was considered an important adjunct of the church service. He says:

"In short there are Germans here, and perhaps the majority, who despise God's Word and all outward good order; who blaspheme the sacraments and frightfully and publicly give scandal. . . . .

---

[26]Sachse, *German Pietists*, p. 22; *Seidensticker, Geschichtsblaetter*, p. 100.
[27]Seidensticker, *Geschichtsblaetter*, p. 100.
[28]Sachse, *German Pietists*, p. 144 (hereafter quoted as G. P.).

"I will here take occasion to mention that many others besides myself, who know the ways of the land, maintain that music would contribute much towards a good Christian service. It would not only attract and civilize the wild Indians, but it would do much good in spreading the Gospel truths among the sects and others by attracting them. Instrumental music is especially serviceable here. Thus a well-sounding organ would perhaps prove of great profit, to say nothing of the fact that the Indians would come running from far and near to listen to such unknown melody, and upon that account might become willing to accept our language and teaching, and remain with people who had such agreeable things; for they are said to come ever so far to listen to one who plays even a reed-pipe (rohr-pfeiffe): such an extraordinary love have they for any melodious and ringing sound. Now as the melancholy, saturnine stingy Quaker spirit has abolished (relegiert) all such music, it would indeed be a novelty here, and tend to attract many of the young people away from the Quakers and sects to attend services where such music was found, even against the wishes of their parents. This would afford a good opportunity to show them the truth and their error.

"If such an organ-instrument (Orgel-werck) were placed in the Swedish church . . . . it would prove of great service to this church.

"If there were music in the church, the young people would consider church-going a recreation.

"The Lord of Hosts . . . . would be praised and honored with cymbal and organ.

"And it may be assumed that even a small organ-instrument and music in this place would be acceptable to God, and prove far more useful than many hundreds in Europe, where there is already a superfluity of such things.

"There are in Europe masters enough who would build such instruments, and a fine one can be secured for 300 or 400 thalers. Then if an experienced organist and musician could be found, and a curious one, who would undertake so far a journey, he would be very welcome here. In case this could not be, if we only had an organ, some one or other might be found who had knowledge thereof." [29]

---

[29]Cf. *The Missive of Justus Falckner of Germantown, Concerning the Religious Condition of Pa. in the Year 1701. Translated by J. F. Sachse.* Found also in *Pa. Mag. of Hist.*, 1897.

The writer of this missive was somewhat of a poet himself, and composed several fine hymns, some of which are in use at the present day.[30]

Whether the appeal for musical instruments was of avail, we know not, but in the *Journal of Rev. Andreas Sandel* for July 20, 1702, is mentioned one Jonas, organist of Gloria Dei church. Again, on November 24, 1703, when Falckner was ordained in this church, Sachse says:

"The service was opened with a voluntary on the little organ in the gallery by Jonas the organist, supplemented with instrumental music by the Mystics on the viol, hautboy, trumpets (*Posaunen*) and kettle drums (*Pauken*)"[31]

The first church organ in Philadelphia, then, was placed in a Swedish Lutheran church largely by means of a German. Although the merit for this achievement must be divided between the Germans and Swedes, in one department of music—the singing of hymns—the Swedes probably were pre-eminent. In 1696 Charles, King of Sweden, sent to the church at Wicacoa, one hundred hymn books,[32] while in 1712 another lot, consisting of "360 hymn books of three sorts" were shipped.[33] The Swedes were strict, too, in the regulations of the church services, epecially of singing. In 1702, Rev. Andreas Sandel imposes a fine "for untimely singing, six schillings."[34] Especially interesting is the account concerning the attempt of Pastor Andreas Hesselius, of Christina, Dlaware, to reform church singing in 1713. Acrelius says:

"He had special regard to propriety in church-singing, in which there was often such discord as though they intended to call their

---

[30]Sasche, *Justus Falckner*, pp. 20-21.

[31]*Justus Falckner*, p. 64; also G. P., pp. 354-5. Sachse believes this organ was one brought over by Kelpius.

[32]Israel Acrelius, *A History of New Sweden, trans. by Wm. Reynolds*, in *Memoirs of Pa. Hist. Soc.*, Vol. XI, pp. 197, 366 (hereafter quoted as Acrelius).

[33]Acrelius, p. 367; also *Andreas Sandel's Diary, in Pa. Mag. Hist.* 1906, p. 446.

[34]Acrelius, p. 217.

cows to the church. In opposition to which it was represented that as all those who possessed the gift of praising God with a pleasing voice in psalms and hymns should not stand mute, so, on the other hand, those who were unfitted for this should not with their harsh voices, hinder others and make confusion, but, by softly singing after the others, train themselves to correct singing. During the singing, he went around the church and aided where they failed."[35]

It is very probable that in Philadelphia, this same instruction in church singing prevailed, since Hesselius was for some time Provost, and had a right to command, and also, because Samuel Hesselius, his brother, occupied the pulpit at Wicacoa and could more easily be coerced—if necessary—to establish this method of instruction.

In the other churches of Philadelphia, organs seem to have been introduced at a relatively late date. On September 2, 1728, a committee having been appointed at Christ Church "to treat with Mr. Lod. C. Sprogel,[36] about an organ lately arrived here, report that they had done the same, and that he insisted on £200 for said organ; and that they had procured men of the best skill this place could afford to erect the said organ in a convenient house in town, to make trial thereof; which, being done, it is said the organ proves good in its kind, and large enough for our church."[37] Upon this recommendation the organ was purchased. In the Moravian church, corner of Race and Broad streets, there were two organs in 1743[38] one of which was sold in 1796, and a new one built by David Tannenberger[39] In this same year (1743) the Moravians in Germantown had an organ costing £60, but in 1744 both church and organ reverted to the German Re-

---

[35]Acrelius, p. 276.

[36]Ludovic Christian Sproegel was one of the "Hermits of the Wissahickon."

[37]Quoted from the *Minutes of the Vestry of Christ Church*, by Benj. Dorr, *History of Christ Church*, p. 61.

[38]Madeira, *Annals of Music in Philadelphia*, p. 24.

[39]Madeira, *Annals of Music in Philadelphia*, p. 24 (hereafter quoted as Madeira).

formed Church.[40] The Catholic church had an organ in 1750.[41] These are the earliest known organs in use in Philadelphia churches. From this time on, the other churches in the city gradually established them as an aid to their services.

One writer, who came to this country from Germany, evidently had no knowledge of these organs when he said:

"I came to this country with the first organ [1750] which now stands in a High German Lutheran church in the city of Philadelphia, and which was built in Heilbronn.[42]

In the face of the evidence already produced, it is needless to say that this statement is a little off color, to say the least.

There were then in Philadelphia several organs before 1755, and it is reasonable to assume that in the Moravian church, that "wind" and "string" instruments were used, since we find this true at the colony in Bethlehem.[43] The testimony of travellers of that time or of members of other churches is of some interest and importance. The first witness is William Black, secretary of the commission appointed by the Governor of Virginia to unite with commissions from Maryland and Pennsylvania for the purpose of treating with the Indians. In the year 1744, he resided in Philadelphia, during which time he kept a journal of interest and importance. June 8 he writes:

"We went to the Moravian Meeting, where I had the pleasure to hear an Excellent Comment on that Passage in Scripture Relating to the Prodigal Son, and after *some very agreeable Church Music,* half an hour after 9 they broke up."[44]

---

[40]*Minutes and Letters of the Coetus of the German Reformed Church,* p. 29.

[41]Madeira, p. 24.

[42]*Gottlieb Mittelberger's Journey to Penn. in the Year* 1750; *translated by Carl T. Eben,* p. 114.

[43]Wm. Reichel, *Something about Trombones,* p. 4 ff. See also the statement concerning Justus Falckner's ordination as quoted above, where musical instruments of this character were used.

[44]*Penn. Mag. of History,* Vol. II, p. 43.

This testimony is not without its value, as this gentleman was evidently somewhat of a musician himself, since under the same date in his diary we find:

"I Rose from my Bed and pass'd two hours in writing, the rest of the time till Breakfast, I spent with my Fiddle and Flute."[45]

Concerning the music in the Moravian church we have other evidence, at a later date. John Adams remarks in his diary for October 23, 1774:

"The singing here [Methodist meeting] is very sweet and soft indeed; the first *music* I have heard in any society *except* the Moravians, and once at church with the organ."[46]

He also remarks September 4, 1774, upon "the organ and a new choir of singers at Christ Church, which were very musical."[47]

Franklin, in 1755, speaks of hearing Moravian music at Bethlehem, and praises it generously.[48] A year earlier Acrelius, who visited the same place, gives a more detailed account in the following words:

"It was finally agreed that we should sit below [in the auditorium of the church], as the music sounded better there. The organ had the accompaniment of violins and flutes. The musicians were back in the gallery, so that none of them were seen." One of the ministers "read some verses of a German hymn book, after which they were sung with excellent music."[49]

Their style of music and manner of performing it must have been exceptionally good, as compared with the music of other churches, to have impressed so favorably such men, who, we may be sure, were quite different. There is the sturdy pastor Acrelius, understanding church music and the manner of its performance; the cordial, genial Ben Franklin, who knew some-

---

[45]*Penn. Mag. of Hist.* Vol. II, p. 40.

[46]*John Adams Works*, Vol. II, pp. 401 and 364.

[47]*John Adams Works*, Vol. II, pp. 401 and 364.

[48]Franklin, *Autobiography*, p. 325 [Lippincott, Phila., 1868].

[49]Acrelius, p. 413.

thing about music from living in London; the somewhat cold but highly cultured, John Adams, with his Puritan traditions; then the gentleman from Virginia, William Black, who most probably partook of the nature of the warm, sunny-tempered Southerners, himself somewhat of a musician. Could we ask for witnesses more unlike?

To the Moravian church undoubtedly belongs the palm for music during the eighteenth century; but there was music, and good music, in some other churches as well. We have already mentioned the music in Christ Church and the Methodist Church. Concerning the music in the German Lutheran Church, we have the testimony of Daniel Fisher, who writes in his *Diary* for May 25, 1755:

"Went to the Lutheran Church, a neat Brick Building where there is a good organ[50] to which I heard them sing Psalms, agreeably enough."[51]

Again he says:

"The Lutheran Church has an organ, and a good one."[52]

There were organs then in the churches, to a great extent, before 1750. The question now arises: Were there men who could repair these instruments if they got out of order? By the end of the fifth decade, there were several men who could not only repair an organ, but also build one. Of these men Gustavus Hesselius is the most important, as he was the first spinet builder in America, having produced specimens as early as 1743,[53] and probably the first organ builder in Pennsylvania. It is claimed that he was the first organ builder in America, and in support of that claim an organ is mentioned as built by him for the Moravian Church at Bethlehem, Pa., in 1746.[54] The fact is lost sight of

---

[50]The organ Mittelberger brought from Heilbronn; see above.
[51]*Penn. Mag. of Hist.*, Vol. XVII, p. 267.
[52]*Penn. Mag. of Hist.*, Vol. XVII, p. 272.
[53]*Penn. Mag. of Hist.*, XVI, p. 473 (note)
[54]*Penn. Mag. of Hist.*, Vol. XXIX, p. 131 ff; also Reichel, p. 4.

that a Boston man, Edward Bromfield, generally regarded as the first organ builder, constructed an instrument in .1745.[55] However Hesselius was undoubtedly the first man who built many church organs.

Still another claimant appears for this title—no less a man than the Englishman, Doctor Christopher Witt (1675-1765), another hermit of the Wissahickon. Doctor Witt possessed a large pipe-organ presumably made by him alone, but possibly aided by other Hermits. It was built at least while he was living with the settlement on the Wissakickon, and as he left that society shortly after the death of Kelpius,[56] which took place about 1708,[57] the evidence is in his favor. This organ at his death was valued at £40.[58]

Hesselius was not only a musician, but a painter as well. He died in 1755.[59] Connected with Hesselius in 1746 was John G. Klemm, a native of Dresden, Germany. Three years later David Tannenberger arrived in Philadelphia, a man whom many of his contemporaries conceded to be the greatest organ builder in America, but, as is usually the case, there is another claimant for this high honor, as will be seen later.

David Tannenberger[59a] was born March 21, 1728, in Berthelsdorf, Saxony. He was evidently an all-round musician, and could play, sing—he possessed a good voice—build, or repair an organ as occasion presented itself. It is known that he built at least fourteen organs during his stay in Pennsylvania, while no record of the number of spinets, which he made and sold for £22.10s, has been discovered.

As to Tannenberger's reputation as an organ builder, we have the testimony of a man who probably knew Tannenberger:

"Tannenberg belongs to history as *the* organ builder of his day and one of renown. He too, was of the German school. Fancy

---

[55]L. Elson, *History of American Music*, p. 43.

[56]*German Pietists*, pp. 403, 412.

[57]*German Pietists*, p. 192.

[58]*German Pietists*, p. 418 (note).

[59]*Penn. Mag. of Hist.*, Vol. XII, p. 503 (note).

[59a]Spelled also Tannenberg.

stops were not generally in vogue, except the trumpet in the great organ, and the vox humana in the swell, of which latter there was but one in the city, and that was in Christ Church, and to my young ear, a good imitation of the human voice.

"There are several of Tannenberg's organs yet in breathing existence [1857]. Lancaster, Litiz, and Nazareth still hold his memory in audible and respectful tones; and much of his work is worthy of imitation. His diapasons were particularly dignified, whilst his upper work, 12th, 15th, and sesquialtera, gave brilliancy to the whole."[60]

This testimony of Abraham Ritter, an organist of good standing in the Moravian Church, gives some idea of the excellence of the work and of the reputation which Tannenberger still had in the nineteenth century.

In a letter written from Lancaster, Dec. 24, 1770, the following testimony is added:

"Yesterday we had the pleasure of hearing, for the first Time, the new Organ, in the High Dutch Reformed church of this Place, accompanied with a variety of vocal Music, composed on the Occasion which I may venture to say, not only from my own Experience, but the Approbation of all present, was never equalled in any Place of Worship in this Province, or perhaps upon this Continent. The Organ was made by Mr. David Tannenberg, of Litiz, a Moravian Town not far from this Place; and I dare venture to assert, is much superior in Workmanship and Sweetness of Sound, to any made by the late celebrated Mr. Feyring, who was so justly taken notice of for his Ingenuity; does great Honour to the Maker; is worth the Attention and Notice of the Curious, who may happen to pass this way; and will undoubtedly recommend him to all who are desirious of having Works of that Nature."[61]

In spite of his reputation as an organ-builder, we learn that in 1790 he was a bankrupt.[62] He died May 19, 1804, stricken by paralysis while tuning an organ at York, Pa.[63]

---

[60]Abraham Ritter, *Hist. of the Moravian Church in Phila.* (1857), p. 59 ff. (note)

[61]*Pa. Gaz.* Jan. 10, 1771.

[62]*General Adv.* Oct. 28, 1790.

[63]*Penn. Mag. of Hist.*, Vol. XXII, p. 231 ff.

We have already spoken of Gottlieb Mittelberger and his organ, and, although we cannot depend upon his statements, there may be some truth in his somewhat exaggerated account of the dedication of his organ. It is at least interesting, and shows that the people as a whole were certainly not prejudiced against music. He says:

"After this work had been set up and tuned it was consecrated with great rejoicing and delivered to the Christian St. Michael's Church for the praise and service of God.

"The crowd of hearers was indescribably large; many people came from a great distance, 10, 20, 30, 40 and even 50 hours' journey, to see and hear this organ. The number of hearers, who stood inside and outside the church, both German and English, were estimated at several thousands. I was appointed school-master and organist. As I became more and more known in Pennsylvania, and the people learned that I had brought fine and good instruments with me, many English and German families came 10, 20 and 30 hours' journey to hear them and the organ, and they were greatly surprised because they had never in all their lives seen or heard an organ or any of those instruments.[64]

"At the present time [1754] there are 6 organs in Pennsylvania —the first is in Philadelphia, the 2nd in Germantown, the 3rd in Providence, the 4th in New Hanover, the 5th in Dulpehocken, all of them came to this country during the four years of my sojourn there."[65]

This statement concerning the number of organs in Philadelphia cannot be true, as we have shown above that there were several. In his list of the organs in Pennsylvania, he neglects to mention the one made for the Moravian Church at Bethlehem in 1746.[66] The number of people which he claims was present at the dedication is probably exaggerated, and, as Mittelberger was the chief performer, we can pardon him this slip of the pen.

---

[64]This statement is utterly false, as it will be shown later that there were musical instruments in Philadelphia long before this time, and even concerts in 1740.

[65]Mittelberger's *Journey to Penn.*, p. 114.

[66]Cf. above, p. 17.

It is probable, however, that there was a large number of people present, as there would be at any new event entering into their narrow lives—especially as there was no charge for admission.

In 1762 a new organ was built in Philadelphia by Philip Feyring for St. Paul's Church. He is the other claimant to the honor of being the greatest organ builder of his day.[67] One of the newspapers was evidently partial to him, since it gives this notice.

"The New Organ, which is putting up in St. Paul's Church in this City, will be in such Forwardness as to be used in Divine Service on Christmas Day. It is of a new Construction, and made by Mr. Philip Feyring,[68] Musical Instrument-Maker, in this City, who may, with Justice, be said to be the best Hand at that ingenious Business on the Continent."[69]

The organ was evidently in use on Christmas day and must have proven satisfactory to call forth the following poem lauding both Feyring and his organ.

"On hearing the Organ at St. Paul's Church, on Christmas Day, 1762.

"Hail Heav'n-born Science! whose enlivening Touch,
Thro' Nature felt, makes all her Powers rejoice,
And fills the Soul with Harmony, and Bliss
Extatic—When Joy tumultuous revels
In the swelling Breast, then thou, sweet Music,
Majestically smooth, and soft as Zephyrs,
The Voice assuasive to the Heart applyst.

"If jarring Passions, like disgorging Etna,
Wage War intestine, and with Rage destroy
Then Mother Nature, instant at thy call
They lose their Fury, and subside in Peace:—
A sov'reign Balm thou pour'st into the Wounds
Of bleeding Love, and sooth'st the Heart-felt Pain.

---

[67]Cf. above, p. 18.
[68]Spelled also Feyring.
[69] *Pa. Gaz.*, Dec. 23, 1762.

And thou, majestic Organ! taught by thee,
We raise our Thoughts on Fancy's Wing,
Soaring beyond the darksome veil of Time
Up to the empyreal Heav'n, where God-head habits,
High thron'd above all Height, encircl'd round
By Seraphims, whose well instructed choirs
To pleasing Numbers tune their Harps of Gold—

"Surely if ought of Heav'n on Earth we taste,
'Tis when we join in holy Acclamation
With deep ton'd Organ, to rehearse the Praise
Of God Omnipotent, who rules the Heav'ns;
When ev'ry swelling Note bears us enraptur'd
To the blest Abodes of Saints imparadis'd.

"When God his six Days Work, a world had finishd
Attended by a Band of heav'nly Music,
The Harp symphonious, and the solemn Pipe
The Dulcimer, all Organs of sweet Stop,
Along the starry Pavement up he rode;
While instant Nature heard the Song harmonious,
And listening Planets ceas'd to fill their Orbs.

"While Harmony divine knows to controul
The boistrous Passions of the human Soul,
Whilst Organ's dulcet Notes the Breast inspire.
With true Devotion, and a sacred Fire;
Thy name O Fyring thy deserving Name
Shall shine conspicuous in the Roll of Fame;
Ages to come, and Men in future Days
Shall greateful pay their Tribute to thy Praise.   C. W. P.

"Mr. Fyring is a German by Birth, but has for some years past, practic'd the making of Musical Instruments (particularly Spinets and Harpsichords) in this City, with great Repute."[70]

This effusion explains itself. His workmanship must have been of superior quality, as it was seldom that a musician at that time—or even at the present day was much noticed, let alone publishing a poem about him.

---

[70]*Pa. Gaz.*, Dec. 30, 1762.

How many instruments were sold by these organmakers it would be difficult to say, although undoubtedly parlor organs were found in many houses. There are advertisements of two organs for sale among a list of household goods before the end of 1750: A "small" organ belonging to Benj. Morgan, 1748,[71] and a "large" one, the property of the late Peter Kook, in 1750.[72]

Religious music in this half century was flourishing, and was considered a valuable adjunct of the church service, not only in German churches, but also in the Swedish and English churches. The composition of hymns up to this time seems to have been confined to the Germans.

---

[71]*Pa. Journal*, July 7, 1748.
[72]*Pa. Journal*, Jan. 2, 1750.

CHAPTER III.

SECULAR MUSIC.

From the preceding chapter it has been clearly seen, that the Germans in Philadelphia, and indeed in the whole State, were strongly religious, and were celebrated for their church music and instrument makers, especially for their organ builders.

Were all the people in Philadelphia as religious as the Germans and Quakers seem to have been, and were there no public amusements? This is an important question, and one not easily answered, especially during the first half of the eighteenth century. It may be thought that this question is not related to German music, but indirectly it is, so that it may be shown whether or not the people of Philadelphia were ready to welcome music, whether they were in a state of mind favorable to the introduction of any amusements. It is necessary to establish these facts before we can clearly understand the reasons and cause for the introduction of German concert music into America.

We know, that in Philadelphia during the eighteenth century, there were men of every creed and religion, of every walk of life, of many different nationalities, and we may be sure that in such a conglomeration of men and ideas there would be some to whom amusements would be necessary—even amusements which strait-laced people would condemn. The information there is upon this subject supports the opinion, that there were amusements even in the early part of the eighteenth century. Foremost among the pleasures in which the inhabitants of Philadelphia indulged, was dancing, and we have reference to this art at an early period. In a book written in 1710 is the following statement:

"Among the rest of my Friends, I must not forget the facetious Mr. Staples, Dancing-Master, who was the first Stranger of Philadelphia that did me the Honour of a Visit." [73]

As early as 1716 we find this record:

"At the Yearly Meeting of the Friends, members were advised against 'going to or being in any way concerned in plays, games, lotteries, music and dancing.'" [74]

Throughout the first half of the eighteenth century dancing was evidently held in due respect by a certain element of the population. In 1728 it forms a part of the curriculum of a boarding school.[75] In 1730 dancing is taught by Thomas Ball's sister.[76] The first really fashionable ball was probably that given by Governor Gordon, in 1726, in honor of the Prince of Wales' birthday.[77] To some extent, too, music and dancing were surely a part of the marriage festivities, as the following item shows:

"We hear that Tuesday night last, a young Dutchman was married to an old Dutchwoman, who was known to have money. They had a fiddle at the Wedding. . . . She danc'd till it was late." [78]

We find ministers of different denominations complaining of the irreligion of some of the inhabitants. As one writer remarks:

"We live in an age, when 'tis counted almost a scandal to be a Christian. Religion is stil'd Preciseness and Hypocrisy, and a strict Conformity to Truth and Virtue is imputed to be the Effect of Melancholy, a Distemper'd Imagination. We daily hear the greatest Mysteries of our Faith Ridicul'd and Banter'd, the Clergy

---

[73]Hart, *American History told by Contemporaries II*, p. 77, quoted from *"The Voyage, Shiprack and Miraculous Escape of Richard Castleman, Gent,"* appended to *"The Voyages and Adventures of Capt. Robert Boyle,"* London, 1726, 4th Ed. 1786, p. 331.

[74]Scharf & Wescott, *History of Phila.*, Vol. II, p. 863.

[75]*American Weekly Mercury*, March 5-14, 172⅞.

[76]*Pa. Gazette*, March 5-13, 1729-30.

[77]Scharf & Wescott, *Hist. of Phila.*, Vol. I, p. 203.

[78]*Pa. Gaz.*, March 15 to 22, 1738-9.

Despis'd, Expos'd and Degraded; and that even by Men, who have not yet Publickly Renounc'd Christianity; but such as would be thought to have clearer Heads, and more refin'd Conceptions of Things than their Brethren, those Men to their Shame stand Pelting Religion at a distance, with little Scoffs and Jests, when there is a more Fair and Honourable way of deciding the Matter, by rational and undeniable Arguments."[79]

In opposition to this we have the testimony of Benjamin Franklin, who writes:

"Our people, having no publick amusements to divert their attention from study, became better acquainted with books."[80]

So, too, a correspondent in the *Weekly Mercury* writes:

"Here are no Masquerades, Plays, Balls, Midnight Revellings, or Assemblies to Debauch the Mind or promote Intrigue."[81]

When, however, we read an advertisement in the same paper about a month later like the following, we may be permitted to doubt somewhat the statements of the last two men.

"The Art of Dancing Carefully Taught (as it is now Practic'd at Court) by Samuel Perpoint, at his *School.* . . . where for the Recreation of all Gentlemen and Ladies: There will be *Country Dances every Thursday Evening*; likewise he teaches small Sword."[82]

From this time on, we notice the advertisements of various dancing masters, who, often were school masters at the same time. Not only did these Philadelphians enjoy dancing, but they were partial to late suppers and card playing as well,—playing cards was a staple article of importation after 1736.[83] Another favorite amusement, we may be sure, was playing on the Jew's harp, for after 1733, this instrument frequently is advertised.[84] The

---

[79]*American Weekly Mercury*, June 19-26, 1729 [a correspondent].
[80]*Autobiography*, p. 207.
[81]*American Weekly Mercury*, June 19-26, 1729.
[82]*American Weekly Mercury*, July 31 to August 7, 1729.
[83]*American Weekly Mercury*, February 8, 1736 [first advertised].
[84]*American Weekly Mercury*, March 2, 1733 [first advertised].

Jew's harp must have been considered a harmless instrument by all sects, for as early as 1675 in one State of Puritan New England it is stated that a law was enacted, "that no one should play on any kind of music except the drum, the trumpet and the jew-sharp."[85]

Besides the amusements already mentioned, the Philadelphians had an opportunity to see a rope-dancer in 1724,[86] "Punch and Joan his Wife,"[87] "Magick Lanthorn'" exhibition,[88] "Camera Obscura and Microscope,"[89] a musical clock with a man and woman appearing as mountebanks.[90]

Music was evidently popular at society meetings, banquets, etc. Perhaps there was nothing more than singing, but possibly a violin and spinet helped to while away the time. For instance, in 1731 at the celebration of "St. David's Day," by the "Society of Ancient Britons," the evening ended with "Musick, Mirth and Friendship."[91]

In the two items which will be given now, may be detected, perhaps, the incipient germs of musical criticism, or at least the idea, which most people probably had of what a professor of music should know and be able to do:

"Elocution is not unlike Musick; there is scarce a Soul so rustick as not to admire both in their Excellency, altho' the Masters of those Sciences may lose their proper Share of the Praise. He that having laid before him the several Parts of a Musical Instrument, can Unite them in their Places, and tune them to Harmony, merits the appelation of a Master in Musick and should be distinguished as such, as he that disposes Words into grammatical sentences, and eloquent Periods, is a Master of Language."[92]

---

[85]Perkins & Dwight, *History of Haendel & Haydn Society*, p. 17 (note).
[86]Scharf & Wescott, Vol. II, p. 863.
[87]*Pa. Gaz.*, Dec. 30, 1742.
[88]*Pa. Gaz.*, Jan. 27, 1743.
[89]*Pa. Gaz.*, July 2, 1744.
[90]*Pa. Gaz.*, May 31, 1744.
[91] *Pa. Gaz.*, Feb. 23 to March 4, 1730-31.
[92] *American Weekly Mercury*, Aug. 7-14, 1729.

This quotation may argue for the popularity and respect in which music was held at that time by at least some of the people. We find in this crude statement, that music was thought worthy of a position by the side of elocution, which has always held a high place in the minds of every people, and so we may be safe in believing that music had a place, and an important place, in Philadelphia, in the early history of that city.

Another correspondent states that:

"Women, like Instruments of Musick, require to be long used before their Sweetness or Discord are certainly discovered."[93]

Unless the writer of the above knew something about music, and unless music was an object of interest or pleasure, so that this comparison would be appreciated, he would not likely have ventured to use such a simile.

In 1733 there is a record of a "ball"[94] while, in the next year under the heading "London news," there is a notice concerning the marriage of the Princess Royal to the Prince of Orange, which gives the following information:

"A fine anthem compos'd by Mr. Handell was perform'd by a great Number of Voices and Instruments."[95]

This latter item proves nothing except that the name of Händel was introduced into the colonies at an early date, and may have remained in the memories of some of the people, since he was connected with such an important event. This may possibly have helped to increase the popularity which his works, later in the century, attained in America.

It has been seen that there was music and dancing at this time, and it is now interesting to learn what kind of musical instruments were used. It has been shown already, that there

---

[93]*American Weekly Mercury*, Sept. 10-17, 1730.
[94]*American Weekly Mercury*, Nov. 11, 1733.
[95] *American Weekly Mercury*, May 23, 1734.

were Jew's harps,[96] that Kelpius had clavichords,[97] and assuredly there were some virginals, although probably few. In the fifth decade the various instrument makers mentioned above,[98] probably had quite a number of customers.

In 1729 Andrew Bradford, proprietor of the *American Weekly Mercury*, advertises:

"A well-strung Virginal to be sold; being in good Order. Enquire of Printer hereof."[99]

Dr. Christopher Witt, referred to before,[100] was a capable player on the virginal,[101] which at his death was appraised at £1, 15s.;[102] while a virginal belonging to the "Hermits" reverted to the widow of Magister Zimmerman.[103]

The people who owned instruments of this kind had an opportunity to learn to play, since in 1730 a woman—the first music teacher in Philadelphia— makes an announcement in the newspaper as follows:

[Thomas Ball's] "Wife teaches Writing and French. Likewise Singing, Playing on the Spinet, Dancing and all sorts of Needle-Work are taught by his Sister lately arrived from London."[104]

What class of music she and her pupils played, it would be hard to say, but it did not cause anyone to start a music store, and it is not until 1739 that any great musical works are advertised at the office of the man of many parts, Benjamin Franklin. The following pieces were to be obtained there: "Corelli's Sonatas, Geminiani's Concertos, Ditto's Solos."[105]

---

[96]*Vide* above, p. 26.

[97]*Vide* above, p. 11.

[98]*Vide* above, p. 17 ff.

[99]*American Weekly Mercury*, March 4-13, 1728-9.

[100]See above p. 18.

[101]*German Pietists*, p. 412.

[102]*German Pietists*, p. 418 (note).

[103]*Justus Falckner*, p. 64 (note).

[104]*Pa. Gaz.*, July 2-9, 1730.

[105]*Pa. Gaz.*, June 15-22, 1738-9.

Besides spinets and virginals there were probably violins, German flutes, trumpets, drums, a few viols, etc. For instance, in 1749 Anthony Lamb, of New York, advertises among other things: "German Flutes,"[106] while other men advertise, in 1750, "Hunting Pipes," [107] and "fiddle strings,"[108] From 1744 on numerous advertisements of drums appear.

Before 1740 there is no record of any kind of musical organization, but in this year there was such a society. During this year the evangelist, Whitefield, visited Philadelphia and made a strong impression upon people of all beliefs. One of his disciples caused this to be printed:

"Since Mr. Whitefield's Preaching here, the Dancing school, Assembly, and Concert Room have been shut up, as inconsistent with the Doctrine of the Gospel: and though the Gentlemen concern'd caus'd the Door to be broke open again, we are inform'd that no Company came to the last Assembly night."[109]

One of the members, however, denied the charge that dances were inconsistent with the doctrine of the gospel, and affirmed that the hall was closed up by William Seward, an "Attendant and intimate Companion" of Whitefield. This same writer speaks of "Members of the Concert" and the rooms belonging to them. He also says that the members "met the Night after according to Custom; and the Thursday following the Company met to Dance as they used to do; but the Assembly being only for the Winter Season is now discontinued of Course and the Concert being for the whole Year still goes on as usual."[110]

This is interesting, as it is the first record of concerts, and also, because these *concerts*, continued the *whole* year, not merely during the winter months as nowadays. There were "Members of the Concert," too, who rented or owned rooms. There must

---

[106]*Pa. Gaz.*, Jan. 31, 1749.
[107]*Pa. Journal*, Jan. 9, 1750.
[108]*Pa. Jour.* and also *Pa. Gaz*, May 24, 1750.
[109]*P. Gazette*, May 1, 1740.
[110]*Pa. Gaz.*, May 8, 1740.

then have been some kind of a club or society, which gave these performances.

These concerts must either have been kept up for years, or new series instituted year by year, since our friend William Black (already quoted) says in his diary of 1744, June 5:

"At 8 O'Clock went to hear a Concert of Musick; the Performers was some Town's Gentlemen, and did Us the Honour of an Invitation, we staid till past 11, and I left the Company to go home to my lodgings."[111]

It is important to observe, that William Black says he had the "Honour" to be invited to a concert. One might say that this word was simply a common expression. It probably was, and still is; but we believe a man would hardly write such an expression in his diary, unless he really thought he was honored. It seems probable that this concert and those of 1740 must have been very exclusive and were not public entertainments, which anyone might attend.

There was exhibited this same year (1744) a curiosity, which would attract a large crowd of people. This was no less than:

"The Unparallelled Musical Clock, made by that great Master of Machinery, David Lockwood. It excels all others in the Beauty of its Structure and plays the choicest Airs from the most celebrated Operas with the greatest Nicety and Exactness. It performs with beautiful graces, ingeniously and variously intermixed, the French Horn, Pieces, perform'd upon the Organ, German and Common Flute, Flageolet, etc., Sonata's, Concerto's, Marches, Minuetts, Jiggs and Scots Airs, composed by Corelli, Alberoni, Mr. Handel and other great and eminent Masters of Musick."[112]

This is the first public record we have, that works of such famous composers were played, and they must have become familiar, in a short time to a great number of inhabitants.

---

[111]*Penn. Mag. of Hist.*, Vol. I, p. 416.
[112]*Pa. Gaz.*, July 12, 1744.

It will be remembered that Miss Ball's capabilities in the province of music were confined to but two branches, voice and spinet. In 1749, however, appears a truly musical genius, if we may judge by the number of instruments which he played. This man was, as we learn from the following:

"John Beals, Musick Master from London [who] at his House in Fourth Street, near Chestnut Street, joining to Mr. Linton's, collar maker, teaches the Violin, Hautboy, German Flute, Common Flute and Dulcimer by Note.
"Said Beals will likewise attend young ladies, or others, that m ay desire it, at their houses. He likewise provides musick for balls o r other entertainments."[113]

Here was an opportunity for the inhabitants of the Quaker City to improve their time by learning music, and as the variety of instruments from which they might choose, was large, no doubt some of them became proficient musicians.

This same year saw the beginnings of drama and opera in Philadelphia, given by the English actors, Murray and Kean.[114] These dramatic performances were soon discontinued on account of the opposition of the public. From now until the latter part of the sixth decade of the eighteenth century there were desultory attempts to give dramas, but not until 1759 did the theatre prove successful and become permanent.

There was then in this decade an incipient appreciation of drama to which some music was oftentimes joined. What other music was there at this time? In 1750-4 Mittelberger says:

"The cultivation of music is rather rare as yet. . . . Some Englishmen give occasional concerts in private houses with a spinet or harpsichord."[115]

Mittelberger's statement concerning the cultivation of music is not quite true. Music undoubtedly was studied a great

---

[113]*Pa. Gaz.*, March 21, 1749.
[114]Madeira, *Annals of Music*, p. 29.
[115]*Mittelbergers Journey*, p. 114 ff.

deal more than Mittelberger seems to think. If his statement that occasional private concerts were given by Englishmen is true, this was probably the kind of concert William Black attended in 1749,[116] and may have been similar to the concerts of 1740.[117]

During the first half of the eighteenth century Philadelphia was not so utterly devoid of musical culture as some of our historians of music would have us believe. The music was not entirely church music, and although musical culture was not so important a factor in the life of the people as at the present day, still music was beginning to make itself felt among intelligent people, and interest in it and appreciation of it were gradually growing.

---

[116]Cf. above, p. 31.
[117]Cf. above, p. 30.

PART II

Period of Progress, 1750 - 1783

CHAPTER IV.

Music Teachers

From the preceding chapters it will be evident that secular music was beginning to be a force in the life of the people although the religious music certainly in the first half of the 18th century was more prominent. From 1750 on, however, secular music gradually but surely replaces religious music to a great extent, and becomes to all intents and purposes the noticeable feature of the musical life of Philadelphia.

The introduction of German concert music strange to say, evidently was not due to Germans, although the various German teachers of music may later have aided in popularizing the music of their native land. Too much credit cannot be given to the different music teachers from England, who inaugurated public concerts in Philadelphia, where the works of the greatest artists of Germany, England, and Italy were produced.

As early as 1729[118] a music teacher appeared in Philadelphia, while in 1749[119] another member of the profession advertises for pupils. From now on this class of men increases, but there is noticeable lack of teachers with German names. The greater part of these men were English; a few French, Italians, and Germans being present also.

In 1755 appears an unique advertisement showing that some of the German music teachers were not dependent upon music alone for a livelihood.

"The subscriber proposes to open a school on Monday next, in the house where the late Mr. Quin[120] formerly dwelt, for the in-

---

[118]See above, p. 29.
[119]See above, p. 32.
[120]Mr. Quin was a dancing-master, and his room is advertised for rent in *Pa. Gaz.*, Sept. 11, 1755.

struction of Gentlemen and Ladies, in the following accomplishments:

"First, The French, Italian and German languages, in a method concise and easy.

"Secondly, To play on the violin after the Italian manner, with a peculiar method of bowing and shifting in solo's or concerto's.

"Thirdly, Drawing and miniature painting with colours, flowers, insects, etc. . . . Likewise to draw patterns for embroidery, or any kind of needle work. . . . .

"He has a variety of music, composed by the most. eminent masters, for the violino solo, con cembalo et violoncello, to be disposed of on easy terms.

John Matthias Kramer."[121]

Five years later another accomplished German music teacher appeared upon the scene, whose modest advertisement is a relief after reading the previous effusion. This man confines himself to the German flute, which seems to have been an instrument of some importance at that period. This notice runs as follows:

"This is to inform the Public,

"That an Evening School for teaching young Gentlemen to play upon the German Flute will be opened by the Subscriber . . . . where young Gentlemen may be taught, by an easy and regular Method, to play with Judgement and Taste, for the moderate Price of Six Shillings per Week, and Thirty Shillings Entrance Money, provided the Subscriber can procure six Scholars. The Hours of Attendance will be every Evening (Sundays excepted.) from 6 to 8 o'clock. Said Subscriber will also attend Gentlemen at their Houses, one Hour every other Day, for one Guinea per Month and Thirty Shillings Entrance.

John Stadler.

N. B. If any Gentleman is desirious to know the character and abilities of said Subscriber as a Teacher of Music, they may be satisfied by enquiring of any Gentleman in this City, who is a Judge of these Matters."[122]

It is to be noted that Stadler opened a *school* for his instrument, which emphasizes the popularity which this instrument must have enjoyed.

---

[121]*Pa. Gaz.*, Nov. 6, 1755.
[122]*Pa. Gaz.*, Aug. 27, 1761.

Two years later another German flutist, George Isenberg or D'E'issenburg[123] increased the force of teachers in Philadelphia. Again we find in 1774 Peter Kalckoffer advertising to teach the beloved German flute as well as the Latin tongue.[124]

Probably the most important of these German musicians was H. B. Victor, who went from Germany to London, in 1759,[125] and whose advertisement appears in 1774—an advertisement worthy to be placed alongside of some of those of the present day. He seems to have been an inventor of musical instruments as well. The number of instruments he plays at once, remind us of some of the street musicians of the present day.

"Mr. Victor, Musician to her late Royal Highness the Princess of Wales, and Organist at St. Georges in London, lately arrived here, takes this method of acquainting the Musical Gentry in general, that he gives instructions on the Harpsichord, or Forte Piano, Violin, German Flute, etc., especially in the thorough Bass both in theory and practice, for that his pupils may soon come to a fundamental knowledge of that fine science.

N. B. Mr. Victor intended to give a concert, and to perform on his new musical instruments, but is obliged to postpone it for want of able hands; the one he calls Tromba doppia con Tympana, on which he plays the first and second trumpet and a pair of annexed kettle-drums with the feet all at once; the other is called cymbaline de amour, which resembles the musical glasses played by harpsichord keys, never subject to come out of tune, both of his own invention. He is to be met with at his house in Callow Hill street near Water street."[126]

According to this advertisement, Victor must have been a whole conservatory of music in himself. However he was a musician of some note in our early history, and as such is worthy a place here.

As would be expected the remainder of this period brings no new teachers to notice as the colonies were busied with far more important matters.

---

[123]*Pa. Gaz.*, May 15, 1763.
[124]*Pa. Jour.*, June 8, 1774.
[125]Sonneck, *Early Secular Amer. Music*, p. 193.
[126]*Pa. Packet*, Oct. 17, 1774.

CHAPTER V.

Music Dealers, Etc.

To supply the needs of his pupils it is necessary for a music teacher either to carry a line of musical wares himself or to satisfy his wants from a merchant dealing in such things. For some time it is quite likely that each teacher imported his own musical merchandise, although it has already been noted that, at an early date, Benj. Franklin had some music on sale.[127] As in every business there is some one ready to grasp an opportunity, so in the music business a man stepped forward to relieve the teachers of buying and selling. This man was Michael Hillegas, who in 1759 opened, what may be called, the first real music store in Philadelphia. A glance at the following advertisement will not belie this claim.

"To be sold by Michall Hillegas, at his House in Second street, opposite Samuel Morris, Esq., an extraordinary good and neat Harpsichord with four stops; a good Violin-cello, an Assortment of English and Italian Violins, as well common ones, as double lined, of which some extraordinary; a parcel of good German Flutes, imported here from Italy. Also imported in the last ships from London, a large Assortment of Musick, of the best Masters, viz.: Solo's, Overtures, Concerto's, Sonata's, and Duets, for Violins, German Flutes, Hautbcys, French Horns, Violoncello's, and Guitars, Voluntaries, Lessons for Organs and Harpischords, ruled paper of various Sorts for Musick, and Musick Books, Tutors or Books of Instructions to learn to play on the Violin, German Flute, Hautboy, or Common Flute, without a Master, Song Books, Cantatas, Songs on Sheets, and a Choice Parcel of Violin Strings, etc."[128]

---

[127]See above, p. 29.
[128]*Pa. Gaz.*, Dec. 13, 1759.

From this advertisement may be deduced many things. In the first place, such an inventory of stock would not be sneered at by a music dealer of the present day; we may be sure then that the people were musical and that there was a demand for the things advertised. We should suppose that violins and German flutes were the most popular instruments and were in great demand; while there was certainly more than one player—perhaps many—of the above, common flute, French horn, 'cello, and guitar; and of course there were organists and harpsichord players.

Thus we are certain, that, in a few years that the people must have progressed rapidly in music, and probably now it was considered a necessary part of every young lady's and young gentleman's education. Music paper, too, is advertised by Hillegas. This may have been used in copying compositions of other writers as we know Hopkinson did,[129] or, perhaps, there were composers at that time of whom there is no record. The song-books, cantatas, and songs imported would be those in favor in London, as musical taste at this period in Philadelphia was a reflection of English taste.

The name of Michael Hillegas will live as long as the United States hold together, as he was an important figure in the early history of our country.

Michael Hillegas[130] was born April 22, [O. S.]——in Philadelphia of German parents. The tradition runs in the Hillegas family that their ancestors were French. They had a court of arms containing three musical staves. However that may be Michael's parents came from Baden and settled in Philadelphia, where Michael Sr. was naturalized April 11, 1749. He was a merchant, and was interested in real estate and prospered exceedingly. At his death Oct. 11, 1749, his property was valued at £40,000 of which his son Michael had two shares.

Michael Jr. now carried on the business of his father. He was popular, devoted to music and a skilful player on the flute and

---

[129]See below, p. 48.
[130]Oldest reliable spelling is Hilde-gras.

violin, and a composer of "An Easy Method for the Flute."[131] As early as 1753, he advertises a church or house organ.[132]

Politically he was important, held various offices in Philadelphia, and upon the adoption of the constitution became treasurer—the first treasurer of the United States—an office which he held throughout the war.[133]

Such in brief was the man who kept the first store of musical merchandise. His influence in musical matters must have been felt, although it cannot be proven. That he had good musical taste or that the public did is seen from the list of standard works which he advertised in 1764[134] including those of Tartini, Hass, Noseri, Alberti, Vincent, Carter, Miller, Balicourt, Tessorini, Reed, Stanley, Viaci, Cervetto, Davis, Quants, Martini, Weideman, Hellendaal, Pepush, Triemer, Wodizka, Corelli, Depuis, Avison, Humphreys, Alcock, Festnig, Händel, Vivaldi Boyce, Ruge, Price, Burney, Fisher, Ferigo, Flackston, Bates, Retzel, Benegger, Bezozsi, Albinoni, Graun, Stamitz, Fritz, Barbella, Richter, Kleinecht, Lampugnini, Pasquali, M'Gibbon, Dottel, Gerard, Stechwey, Battino, Campioni, Claget, Agzell, Figlio, Diragini, Lanzetti, Kunzen, Scarlatti, Smith [Schmidt?], Barbandt, Berg. This is a list of names of composers which, at that time were popular and some of which hold an important place in the musical world of to-day.

Although Michael Hillegas, probably for some time, had almost a monopoly of the selling of musical merchandize, it was not long before another firm usurped the position which Hillegas had held in the musical world, and apparently crowded him out of business, as his advertisements, after a short time, are few and gradually cease altogether. The music-house par excellence which now came to the front was that of the English book-sellers, Rivington & Brown.

---

[131]Advertised in *Pa. Gaz.*, June 19, 1776.

[132]*Pa. Gaz.*, Aug. 9, 1753.

[133]Material for this sketch taken from "*Michael Hillegas and His Descendants*" by Emma St. Clair Whitney; also, "*A Memoir of the First Treasurer of the U. S,*" by M. R. Minnich.

[134]*Pa. Gaz.*, Jan. 5, 1764.

who carried a remarkably large stock of musical merchandize. [135]However we are only concerned with those storekeepers of German descent so we will have to pass by this large and prosperous establishment.

Soon after this Theodore Memminger, a liquor dealer, advertises:

"A Fine Parcel of Violins, at a very low Price. They are all made by the best Masters in High Germany. He has likewise the best Sort of Fiddle Strings." [136]

In 1768 he seems to have increased his music business, as the following notice shows:

"A Variety of violins at different prices; the best kind of fresh fiddle strings: guitar and spinnett brass and steel wire: a fine pair of very good ivory German flutes. He spins all sorts of bass strings with silver wire," [137]

Most of this business seems to have been in the hands of the English for with the exception of one more German Conrad Batis, who advertises among other things "a quantity of violins and violin strings," [138] no other German music dealer has been discovered.

There is, however, one more event of importance to chronicle, before leaving the music dealers. It has been already stated that harpsichords and spinets were made in Philadelphia at an early period. It remained for John Behrent, a German, to add to the renown of Philadelphia in the realm of music. In 1775 he advertised:

"John Behrent, Joiner and Instrument Maker living in Third street continued in Campington, directly opposite Coate's Burying-ground, Has just finished for sale, an extraordinary fine instrument, by the name of Piano Forte, of Mahogany, in the manner of an harpsichord, with hammers, and several changes: He intends to dispose of it on very reasonable terms: and being a master of such sort of work, and a new beginner in this country he requests all lovers of music to favour him with their custom, and they shall not only be

---

[135]Cf. *Pa. Gaz.*, Feb. 4. 1762, also *Pa. Jour.*, Dec. 15, 1763.
[136]*Pa. Gaz.*, Nov. 10, 1763.
[137]*Pa. Jour.*, Nov. 17, 1768.
[138]*Pa. Gaz.*, Feb. 17, 1773.

honestly served, but their favours gratefully acknowledged, by their humble servant, John Behrent."[139]

Evidently the War of the Revolution interrupted any further progress in musical development, as nothing more of importance is found during this period.

---

[139]*Pa. Pack.*, Mar. 13, 1775.

CHAPTER VI.

CONCERT MUSIC.

In a previous chapter it was shown that a kind of subscription concert was given as early as 1744, and although there is no record of public or private concerts being given for sometime after that, it is only natural to suppose that at least private chamber concerts were given.

We may be sure that bands were a feature at an early date, and no doubt added somewhat to the musical life of Philadelphia. It is not until 1755, however, that there is any mention of such an organization. However in that year we learn that a "Band of Musick" headed a procession of Masons on St. John's Day.[140] How important this procession was considered by the onlookers is seen from the testimony of Daniel Fisher who writes in his diary:

"I should observe that on St. John the Baptist Day (June 24) there was the Greatest Procession of Free Masons to the Church and their Lodge, in Second Street that was ever seen in America. No less than 160 being in the Procession in Gloves, Aprons, etc., attended by a band of Music."[141]

This band probably was not like those of the present time, but may have been satisfactory to the inhabitants of old Philadelphia. We may assume it was similar to a drum and fife corps, although this assumption may do injustice to the musical taste of that time. Anyway we have the year following a more detailed description of a procession including music.

---

[140]*Pa. Gaz.*, Jun. 26, 1755.
[141]*Pa. Mag. of Hist.*, Vol. XVII, p. 273.

"The Philadelphia Regiment consisting of upwards of 1,000 able-bodied men after being reviewed and performing the Manual Exercises [went] thro' the Town in Three Grand Divisions. . . . with Hautboys and Fifes in Ranks.. . . [and] Drums between the third and fourth Ranks."[142]

This is certainly a small beginning but the band had come to stay and apparently was popular, and prabably was used in most processions and public celebrations.   After the victory at Louisburg fireworks were displayed in Philadelphia and a performance of a "Band of Music playing Britons strike home."[143]

At a later date bands of the British regiments stationed in Philadelphia, aided at the public commencements of the "College and Charity School"[144] now the University of Pennsylvania.

The year 1757 is very important in the history of music in Philadelphia.   We have now the "first *public* concerts on record," says O. G. Sonneck.[145]   The advertisement runs:

"By particular Desire.   On Tuesday next, the 25th instant, at the Assembly Room, in Lodge Alley will be performed a Concert of Music, under the direction of Mr. John Palma,[146] to begin exactly at Six o'clock.   Tickets to be had at the London Coffee House, at one Dollar each, and no Person to be admitted without a ticket."[147]

Another concert was given March 25th, of this same year.[148] This year, too, a man appears in musical circles, who undoubtedly exercised more influence upon musical affairs in Philadelphia than any one man before or since.   This is no other than Frances Hopkinson, statesman, signer of the Declaration of Independence, Lawyer, Writer, Inventor, Composer of Music, etc., etc.   His contributions to the music and musical taste of this country is little known, but

---

[142]*Pa. Journal*, Mar. 2-5, 1756.
[143]*Pa. Gaz.*, Sept. 7, 1758.
[144]*Pa. Gaz.*
[145]Cf. O. G. Sonneck, *Frances Hopkinson and James Lyon.*
[146]Palma was formerly a music teacher in London.
[147]*Pa. Gaz.*, Jan. 20, 1757.
[148]*Pa. Journal*, Mar. 24, 1757.

when we say that the evidence points to him as the first native composer in America, although Jas. Lyon of this city may have been—they both wrote music as early as 1759[149]—this fact makes him a man of the greatest importance in musical circles. We wish to correct here a statement made by various writers on American music, that William Billings was the first American composer. This is absolutely false, since Hopkinson and Lyon composed music at least ten years before Billings did, while the latter was yet a child.

It will not be out of place here to give a short account of Frances Hopkinson, laying particular stress upon his musical labors, especially as regards German music.

Frances Hopkinson was born in Philadelphia, Sept. 21, 1737, the son of Thomas and Mary Hopkinson. He must have been keen, active, and studious, since, while yet a boy of twenty, he received his degree with the first class ever graduated from the College of Philadelphia. From now on he advanced in knowledge and in favor with the world. In 1760 he received the degree of Master of Arts from his Alma Mater, and in 1763 recieved the same degree from the College of New Jersey. In 1790 his own college conferred upon him the degree of Doctor of Laws.

His public life was too active to give more than the briefest sketch. His first public office was that of secretary to the governor in a conference between the latter and the Lehigh Indians. From now on, he held many offices, as secretary of the Library Company in 1759; 1772 Collector of the Port of New Castle; 1774 held a seat in Provinicial Council of New Jersey; 1776 delegate to the Continental Congress; signer of the Declaration of Independence; 1779 Judge of the Admiralty from Pennsylvania; 1778 Trustee of the College of Philadelphia. Besides this, he wrote many political pieces of which "The Battle of the Kegs," 1778, was the most popular. He was also for a time organist in Christ Church, instructor in psalmody, a pillar of the church, and an inventor of improvements for the harpsichord.[150]

---

[149]Cf. Sonneck, "*Frances Hopkinson, etc.*" [An admirable discussion.]
[150]Cf. E. P. Cheney, *History of U. of P.*, p. 288 ff.
Also Cf. Sonneck, "*Frances Hopkinson*, etc.

Our first knowledge that Hopkinson studied music is a notice in the magazine containing his "Ode on Music," which remarks:

"Written at Philadelphia by a young Gentleman of 17, on his beginning to learn the Harpsichord.[152]

The only professional music master at that time was John Beals,[153] but, later, 1757, came John Palma[154] and in 1763 James Bremner.[155] Hopkinson may have taken lessons from any or all of these men for all we know to the contrary; but it is certain that he was a pupil of Jas. Bremner, a Scotch musician of some note.[156]

Hopkinson made his first public appearance as a musician probably in 1757 when the "Masque of Alfred"—words by Thompson-Mallett; music by Dr. Arne—was given at the College of Philadelphia as an exercise in oratory.[157] He may have been accompanist for this performance.

It is interesting to note with what music Hopkinson was acquainted at this time and for this purpose I shall quote from Sonneck's exhaustive work:

"The torso of a book with the memorandum 'Frances Hopkinson, 1755,' attracts our attention. It is in manuscript, possibly of the owner. Most pieces have a figured base, and are Italian, French, English trios, songs, and duets, arranged for the harpsichord, amongst them for instance 'A Song in the Triumph of Hibernia,' an 'Air in Atalanta' by Händel, and a famous 'Water Piece' by the same author."[158]

Another book of manuscript bearing the date, 1759, contains pieces by "Händel with *ten* pieces (Samson, evidently being Hopkinson's favorite oratorio by the master), 'Signor Palma,' and 'Signor

---

[152]*American Magazine*, Oct. 1757.
[153]Cf. Above, p.   There was however a music *mistress* Cf. above, p.
[154]Cf. Above 9.
[155]*Pa. Gaz.*, Dec. 1, 1763.
[156]Sonneck, *Frances Hop.* etc., p. 29.
[157]Sonneck, *Frances Hop.*, etc., p. 22 and 40, *Pa. Gaz.*, Jan. 20, 1757.
[158]Sonneck, "*Fr. Hop.*, etc.," p. 32.

Vinci' both with four: Arne with two; Pepush (Alex's a Cantata!) Dr. Boyce, Pergolesi, and Purcell with one piece."[159]

A third volume called "Lessons", date not given, contains, among others, compositions by: "Händel 'who (*predominates*,) Scarlatti, Abel, Stamitz, Vivaldi, Galuppi, Pugnani, Stanley, Smith, [Schmidt], Pasquali, Giardini, Corelli, Geminiani, Lord Kelly."[160]

From these manuscripts it will be seen that Hopkinson was familiar with many of the best composers of the world. He was evidently especially fond of Italian and English composers, but we may judge that he liked Händel's music best of all. In the list directly above there are mentioned the following Germans: Händel, Abel, Stamitz, Schmidt; also the Englishman, Stanley, was a particular friend of Händel, and his music, as was all music of England at that time, must have been modeled after Handel's; then there is Lord Kelley who studied music in Germany. We believe that the greater part of this music was brought to Hopkinson's attention by the music-masters from London, and if that is so, it naturally follows that others of their pupils became acquainted with standard composers. We may be sure, too, that Händel, who was almost idolized in England during this century, had impressed these English American music-masters with his importance, and they would not keep to themselves their knowledge of him and his works. Händel, says one writer:

"For nearly a century . . . stood to the English school as a model of everything that was good and great, to such an extent that very little of original value was accomplished in that country, and when, by lapse of time and a deeper self-consciousness on the part of English musicians, this influence had begun to wane, a new German composer came in the person of Felix Mendelssohn Bartholdy, who, in turn, became a popular idol, and for many years a barrier to original effort."[161]

To turn again to Hopkinson we find that he not only had manuscript books of music, but also printed works such as:

---

[159]Sonneck, *Fr. Hop., etc.*," p. 33.
[160]Sonneck; "*Fr. Hop., etc.*," p. 34.
[161]W. S. B. Matthews. *A Popular History of Music*, p. 281.

"Six Sonatas for the Piano Forte or Harpsichord, Composed by Frederick Theodor Schumann, Opera 5th *London*.[162]

"Händel's Songs selected from the Oratorios."[162]

Then there were books by Italian composers, with which we are not concerned.[162]

From the evidence already presented, it will probably be granted that, the German concert music which was found in Philadelphia in the early 18th century, was brought in rather by the English musicians than by the Germans. We find the taste for music in London reflected by the various music teachers, and by the actors who came to Philadelphia from London during the sixth and seventh decades. This English influence lasted until the War of the Revolution during which there was a period of quiescence. After peace was restored, the English, Germans, and French—the latter exiles and victims of the French Revolution—all aided in the continuance of high class music.

Subscription concerts or in fact concerts of any kind seem to have gone out of fashion in Philadelphia, but in 1764 there was an awakening and a series of concerts was instituted, beginning January the nineteenth; "to be continued every other Thursday, till the 24th of May following. No more than 70 Subscribers will be admitted, and each, on paying Three Pounds for the Season, to have one Lady's Ticket to be disposed of every Concert Night, as he thinks proper."[163]

This then was a series of subscription concerts and must have been confined to the aristocracy of the town. The next year another series of such concerts was given,[164] so they were evidently quite successful. Of these concerts there has been no program discovered, but in the spring of 1765 there is a program of a concert, which is probably representative of the programs given at that time. The advertisement for this concert is of interest:

"On Wednesday evening the 10th Instant at the College Hall in this City was performed a solemn Entertainment of Music under the

---

[162]Sonneck, *Fr. Hop.*, etc., p. 34.

[163]*Pa. Gaz.*, Jan. 12, 1764.

[164]*Pa. Gaz.*, Nov. 1, 1764.

Direction of Mr. Bremner;[165] interspersed with Oratorios, by some of the young Students. . . . . Nearly One Hundred and Thirty Pounds was raised for the Benefit of the Charity Schools belonging to the said College."[166]

The program included overtures of Stamitz, Kelly, and Arne, and Martini, and a concerto of Geminiani; also, sacred songs, orations, and a violin solo.

Besides these exhibitions there were probably concerts of chamber music, as witness:

"Even in the last century [18th] it was usual for families to have meetings at their houses for their improvement in music. Governor Penn, who played the violin, had musical soirees every Sunday evening at his house in South Third Street, during a portion of the year. Dr. Adam Kuhn, himself an amateur, attended them."[167]

The first definite mention of an orchestra was in 1767 when it was announced that the singing in the Southwark Theatre was "accompanied by a Band of Music." [168]"An estimate as to this orchestra is herewith given: violins, flute, harpsichord, oboe, 'cello, trumpet, and, perhaps, French horn and drum.

There were sparks in the town, who also, indulged in serenading their lady loves, an account of which is given by *an Englishman* in a letter to his sister:

"Dear Sister, . . . Pray (as old Polonious says) when you 'was young and in love,' did you approve of serenading? It is extremely in vogue here now. The manner is as follows: We, with four or five young officers of the regiment in barracks, drink as hard as we can, to keep out the cold, and about midnight sally forth, attended by the *band*, which consists of ten musicians, horns, clarinets, hautboys, and bassoons, march through the streets, and play under the window of any lady you choose to distinguish; which they esteem a high compliment. In about an hour all the blackguards who sleep upon the bulks, with gentlemen of a certain profession who sweeten the streets at night, are collected round, drawn by that

---

[165]Cf. Above, p.
[166]*Pa. Gaz.*, Apr. 18, 1765.
[167]W. G. Armstrong, *Record of the Opera in Phila.*, p. 6.
[168]*Pa. Gaz.*, Sept. 24, 1767.

charm which soothes a savage breast, and altogether make it extremely agreeable in a fine frosty morning."[169]

In this letter are mentioned clarinets and bassoons, instruments
possibly not common in Philadelphia. The band probably belonged
to the regiment of which the writer was a member, and was very
small compared to the regimental bands of to-day.

That there could not have been many professional musicians
in Philadelphia is shown by a notice concerning the Southwark
Theatre in 1769:

"The Orchestra on Opera Nights, will be assisted by some musical
Persons, who as they have no View, but to contribute to the Entertainment of the Public, certainly claim a Protection from any Manner
of Insult."[170]

Evidently at this early period people were beginning to be
critical, and, as the orchestra did not come up to their expectations,
they did not hesitate to show their resentment.

It has been said that no concerts are to be traced in Philadelphia
in 1766 and 1767.[171] In 1767 however, Mr. Garner, a teacher of
psalmody advertises four charity concerts,[172] upon which a little
light is thrown by the following notices given by Mr. Garner concerning one of these concerts:

"The vocal parts by Mr. Wools, Miss Wainwright, and Miss
Hallam. The greatest care shall be taken to render the entertainment pleasing and satisfactory."[173]

The program not being in existence, we cannot say with a surety
what character it assumed. It may have been partly of a sacred
character, but it is also likely, since the three singers mentioned
belonged to the theatre, that the program had at least a semi-worldy
tinge.

In 1767 arrived in Philadelphia an Italian, John Gualdo, who
exercised, for a few years, a great influence upon the musical taste

---

[169]*Pa. Mag. of Hist.*, Vol. XI, p. 281.
[170]*Pa. Gaz.*, Nov. 30, 1769.
[171]Cf. Sonneck, *Early Concert Life.*
[172]*Pa. Journ.*, Jan. 8, 1767.
[173]*Pa. Chronicle*, Feb. 2, 1767.

of the people. His choice of music was not limited to compositions of Italian masters, nor to his own compositions, since one of his advertisements states, that the instrumental music is "by Messieurs Geminiani, Barbella, Campioni, Zanetti, Pellegrino, Abel, Bach, Gualdo, the Earl of Kelley, and others."[174]

Sonneck dates Gualdo's first concert Nov. 16, 1769,[175] but according to the following advertisement it would seem to have taken place a month earlier:

"To The Public:
"At the Assembly Room, on next Wednesday (being the 18th of October) will be performed a concert of vocal and instrumental music, for the Benefit of a little Master, not seven years old, who will give a specimen of his early abilities.—The concert to be directed by Mr. Gualdo, after the Italian Method. Tickets at a Dollar a piece. . . . After the Concert, the company (if agreeable) shall be furnished with a set of players, without any expences, in order to end the evening with a ball."[176] Handbills were distributed giving the program.

In his next concert, Nov. 16, two of his performers were Germans, if we may judge from the names. Mr. Curtz played the harpsichord, while Mr. Hoffman Jr., was a clarinet soloist.[177] Another concert not noted by Sonneck was to be given after the races on Sept. 27, 1770.[178] In his next advertisement Gualdo gives a list of the instruments to be used in his next concert, as follows: violins, German flutes, French horns, clarinet, harpsichord, and mandolin.[179] In 1771 Gualdo gave his last concert. This same year is important as it brings to our notice a German, Philip Roth, who was, perhaps, the first *German* composer of secular music in Philadelphia. This first piece was composed for the following concert:

"By Permission and particular Desire,
For the Benefit of Mr. John McLean(Instructor of the German Flute). Will be performed, at the Assembly Room, in Lodge Alley,

[174]*Pa. Jour.*, Nov. 30, 1769.
[175]Sonneck, *Early Concert Life*, etc., p. 71.
[176]*Pa. Chron.*, Oct. 16, 1769.
[177]Cf. Program in Sonneck's, *Early Concert Life*, p. 31.
[178]*Pa. Jour.*, Sept. 27, 1770.
[179]*Pa. Chron.*, Oct. 8, 1770.

A Concert of Music, Vocal and Instrumental: To begin precisely at Six o'clock in the Evening. On Thursday the Fifth of December.

The Concert will consist of two Acts, commencing and ending with favourite Overtures, performed by a *full Band* of Music, with Trumpets, Kettle Drums, and every Instrument that can be introduced with Propriety. The Performance will be interspersed with the most pleasing and select Pieces composed by approved Authors; and a Solo will be played on the German Flute, by John M'Lean, and the whole will conclude with an *Overture, composed* (for the Occasion) by *Philip Roth*, Master of the Band, belonging to his Majesty's Royal Regiment of North British Fusileers, etc."[180]

From this advertisement it will be seen that there must have been an orchestra or band of some importance at this time, and it is quite probable that the British regiments which at various times were stationed in Philadelphia, were important factors in extending the love of music, by means of concerts which the regimental bands must have given.

In 1772 a concert program of little interest was given at the state-house,[181] and in 1774 one by Sigr. Sodi.[182] In a previous chapter was mentioned H. B. Victor, and the concert he intended to give.[183]

The War of the Revolution soon dawned, and with it matters of a serious nature engaged the minds of the people, although occasionally a ball was given, and perhaps regimental concerts. The play houses, which for over ten years, had been an important feature, and had been well patronized by Philadelphians, were closed in 1778 by Act of Congress, but, nevertheless, there was given occasionally a farce or concert.[184] Still music and drama were almost at a standstill during the war.

---

[180]*Pa. Gaz.*, Nov. 28, 1771.
[181]*Pa. Gaz.*, Aug. 19, 1772.
[182]Sonneck, *Early Concert Life*, p. 76.
[183]Cf. Above, p. 39.
[184]Madeira, *Annals of Music*, p. 33.

PART III

Period of Greatest Development (1783-1800)

CHAPTER VII.

ALEXANDER REINAGLE.

During the Revolutionary War it has been stated, that concert music was at a premium. However in the fall of 1783 was founded by John Bentley, the City Concert, "which was an important step in the musical life of Philadelphia." These concerts were to be given every two weeks. As no programs have been preserved, we are unable to determine just what music was used. As Sonneck says: "It goes without saying that John Bentley engaged the best musicians to be had in the city and that he performed music in keeping with the refined taste of such men as Francis Hopkinson and Thomas Jefferson."[185] These concerts were evidently kept up until the season of 1785-6.

In 1786 a musician arrived in Philadelphia, who was of great importance to the musical life of that time. This was Alexander Reinagle one of the ablest musicians in America in that century.

He was born in 1765 at Portsmouth, England, of Austrian parents.[186] He seems to have inherited, as did his brothers Joseph and Hugh, a love of music from his father, who was a skilful musician. Alexander studied music in Scotland with Raynor Taylor, who later became one of the leading musicians in Philadelphia. The material concerning Reinagle before his arrival in America is scanty, but the few data there are show that he was known to the musical world of that time. In a memorandum book[187] of his, preserved in the

---

[185]Sonneck, *Early Concert Life*, p. 79.

[186]Sonneck, *Quarterly Magazine of International Music Society*, October-December, 1906, p. 112.

[187]O. G. Sonneck first called attention to this book in his article in the *Quarterly Magazine of the International Music Society* quoted above p. 113.

Library of Congress, is an account of a trip which he took to Lisbon 1784-5 in company with his brother Hugh, an eminent 'cellist,[188] who was sick with consumption.   They arrived in Lisbon the twenty-third of October, and Reinagle tells of their lodgings there, expenses, etc.   Of special interest is an item for January, 1785:

"Had a Concert in the Assembly Room 8th Jany.—Performed to the Queen and R. family Sunday 16th July. Rec'd. a present from her Majesty of 50 Moids."

After burying his brother Hugh, who died the nineteenth of March, 1785, he "embarked from Lisbon Sat. 23d April sail'd 24th & arrived in Portsmouth Tuesday 17th May.   Made in Lisbon:

By Concert	£100—..—..
By Queen	67—..—..
Two P. Fortes	30—..—..
Four Ditto (?)	35—..—..
Teaching	3—12—..
Fund (?)	31—10—..
	267 2 ..
Expences At Murrays	£7—...—..
Medicines	23—
Diet from 15 Mar. to 23d April at Mrs. Morleys	51
In all Diet	£58
Medicines	23
	81

From these statements it would appear that his trip financially was a decided success.   It would seem from the large sums of money obtained from his performances at Lisbon, that he must have been well known as a prominent musician.   There is further evidence of his standing in the musical world disclosed by O. G. Sonneck in an article in the *Quarterly Magazine of the International Music Society*,"

---

[188]Cf. Articles on Hugh Reinagle, in Grove's *Dictionary of Music*, and in "*Dictionary of National Biography*."

entitled "Zwei Briefe C. Ph. Em. Bachs an Alex. Reinagle." They were evidently good friends, as Bach writes:

"Monsieur

Je Vous suis infinement obligé du Souvenir dont Vous m' honorez et je souhaite que Vous veuillez me le conserver toujours; et dans le cours de vos années les plus riantes. La nouvelle que Vous me donnez de la triste situation de Mr. Vôtre Frère m'a chagriné beaucoup; tant par rapport à Vous qu'à lui même. Le Ciel Vous comble de prospérités, une de plus chères c'est la santé même.

Je Vous envoye la musique, que Vous m'avez demandé, le prix est fixé au prix ordinaire, la musique que je Vous ai donné pour vous même, à Hamburg étoit fixée au prix de premuneration, en Vôtre faveur. Quand Vous m'écrivez une autre fois, ne manquez pas de me marquer Vôtre sort, auquel je m'interesse beaucoup. En même temps je Vous prie de me faire avoir vôtre portrait et celui de Mr. vôtre frère, seulement en dessin, pour les placer dans mon cabinet de portraits des musiciens. Cela me servira d'aide dans le souvenir de vôtre amitié, dans le retour de laquelle ji suis et serai toujours.

Monsieur

Vôtre
trés humble Serviteur.

Hamburg
    ce 25 du mois de Fevrier 1785.   Ch. Ph. Em. Bach.

The other letter is without date, but Sonneck conjectures that it was written the last of 1785 or the beginning of 1786. It runs as follows:

"Liebwehrtester Freund,

Ich bedaure von Herzen den Verlust Ihres lieben und braven Herrn Bruders eben so sehr, als ich mich über Ihre gute Aufnahme in Lissabon und glückliche Wiederkunft in London gefreut habe. Ihr Project wegen meiner gedruckten Rondos kann mir in der Folge viel Schaden thun, weil meine mit grossen Kosten von mir in starken Auflagen verlegten Samlungen, worin sie stehen, unverkauft liegen bleiben werden. Die Liebhaherey zu den Rondos ist hier eben so gross, wie in London, und ich habe sie deswegen mit eingemischt, um meinen Verkauf zu befördern. Ich weiss aus der Erfahrung, dass sehr viele meine Samlungen blos wegen der Rondos kaufen. Folglich sind mir Exemplare von Ihren verlegten Rondos nichts nutze, sondern ich wünschte lieber, dass sie gar nicht nach Deutschland kämen, ohngeacht Westphal hier und Hummel in Berlin ganze Quantitäten von Ihnen würden kommen lassen. Ich will jedoch Ihnen, da Sie etwas damit zu verdienen glauben, einen

Weg vorschlagen, wodurch Sie zu Ihrem Endzwecke kommen könnten, ohne einen Nachdruck befürchten zu dürfen. In der zweiten, dritten, vierten und fünften Samlung stehen überhaupt Rondos. Von diesen Samlungen haben Sie 4, aber die 5, glaube ich haben Sie noch nicht, und kann sie Ihnen, weil 2 Rondos darin stehen, überschicken. Zu diesen 11 Rondos will Ihnen noch 4 neue Rondos componieren; Ich will zufrieden seyn, dass Sie mir Erlaubnis zu dem Drucke dieser schon gedruckten 11 Rondos öffenthich kundthun; und endlich müssen Sie auch bekannt machen, dass ich ausdrücklich für Sie noch nene Rondos dazu gemacht habe. Diese 15 Rondos können Sie in 4 oder wenigern Abtheilungen herausgeben. Es muss aber in jedem Theile etwas neues davon stehen. Dieses Mittel und meine öffentliche Erlaubnis sichert Sie gewiss vor einem Nachdruck.

Für meine Schadloshaltung und für meine neu dazu gekommenen Composition verlange ich nicht mehr und nicht weniger als 34 Guinees. Ich verspreche Ihnen zugleich, dass ich die 4 neuen Rondos niemanden geben noch viel weniger drucken lassen will. Ich kann Ihnen versichern dass 1 Theil von meinen Samlungen, worin nur 2 Rondos vorkommen, nach Abzug aller Kosten, mir wenigstens 1000 Mark hiesiges Geld bisher eingebracht haben, ohne einige 100 Exemplare zu rechnen, die ich noch vorräthig habe, und welche nach und nach auch verkauft werden. Die Auslieferung meiner 4 neuen Rondos auf einmahl geschiehet zugleich bey der Bezahlung auf einmahl. Wir sind sterbliche Menschen. Wegen der Fantasien künftig oder mündlich ein mehreres. Eine baldige genugthuende Antwort mit Ja! oder Nein! elbitte ich mir.

Mit vielen Grüssen verharre ich Ihr Freund und Diener.

Bach.

Hier in Deuschland hat mir noch niemand etwas nachgedcrukt; ich würde auch so gleich in den Zeitungen einen solchen Nachdrucken öffentlich als einen Betrüger erklärt haben, Dafür hält man hier durchgehends einen solchen Menschen, und das will Keiner wagen. Meine öffentliche Eerlaubnis zu Ihrem Drucke und die neuen eingemischten Rondos würden ganz gewiss einen Nachdruck zu Ihrem Schaden abhalten."[189]

These letters merely show that Reinagle before coming to this country was a capable musician, was known as such by prominent musicians in Europe, and probably through his intimacy with Bach would have studied quite extensively the compositions of German musicians.

---

[189]The originals are deposited in the Library of Congress.

It was in the year 1786 that Reinagle arrived in New York with the intention of settling. He inserted the following advertisement in the *New York Independent Journal:*

"Mr. Reinagle, member of the Society of Musicians in London, gives lessons on the pianoforte, harpsichord and violin."[190]

Evidently he did not prosper according to his expectations in New York, since the same year he established himself in Philadelphia. He at once became identified with the musical life of this city, and in conjunction with H. Capron, W. Brown and A. Juhan, Reinagle continued the "City Concerts" instituted in 1783.[191] The first programme played in that year will give some idea of the taste of the people of that epoch.

FIRST CONCERT, OCT. 19, 1786.

Act I.

Favorite Symphonie.................................Vanhall
Song, Mr. Capron.....................................Gretrey
Sonata, Piano Forte.....................Haydn and Reinagle

Act II.

Concerto Flute.......................................Windling
A Favorite Ronde.
Solo Violoncello..Tilliere

Act. III.

Concerto Violin..Cramer
New Symphony................................. Haydon[192]
Miscellaneous Concerto.

It will be seen by this programme that German music had its share of importance, and in later concerts the compositions of Mozart, Haydn, Händel, Bach, Pleyel, Abel, Stamitz, Schmittbauer Heimberger, etc., were given. Undoubtedly the high grade of these concerts and the predominance of the works of German composers, was due to the musical taste of Reinagle.

---

[190]Quoted from *History of the Pianoforte in America*, by Daniel Spillane.
[191]Sonneck, *Early Concert Life*, p. 78.
[192]Quoted from ditto, p. 81.

It is not our intention here to give all the programs which were performed in Philadelphia during this period. Our intention is, however, to give new material which has hitherto not been published. The "City Concerts" Sonneck has traced through the year 1788, and then he adds that "apparently the City Concert was then discontinued as no further reference to it is made until the attempted revival in 1792."[193]

Although no records have as yet been found, still it seems very probable that these concerts were continued without interruption through 1789-90. For the year 1791 there is a complete file of the programs given. The opening announcement is as follows:

"The first Concert will be held on Saturday the 22d instant, at the New-Rooms in Chestnut street, where they will be continued every other Saturday during the Season."

PLAN OF THE FIRST CONCERT.

Act I.

1. Grand Overture of Haydon, Opera 51
2. Song, by a young Lady, composed by Dr. Boyce
3. Solo on the Clarinet,............................Mr. Wolff
4. Quartet of..Pleyel
5. Concerto on the Grand Piano Forte................Miss Moller

Act II.

1. New Overture of................................Haydon
2. Song, by a young Lady, composed by........A. Reinagle
3. Concerto Violin...........................Master Duport
4. Duett, Grand Piano Forte and Violoncello,..............
   Mr. Moller and Amateur
5. Finale of.....................................Dalisac[194]

SECOND CONCERT, FEB. 5.

Act I.

1. Overture ....Pleyel

---

[193]Sonneck, *Early Concert Life*, p. 87.
[194]Cf. *American Daily Adv.*, Jan. 19, 1791.

2. Song...Mr. Wolff
3. Concertante.......................................Cambini
4. Sonato on the Grand Piano Forte............Miss Moller
5. Concerto Clarinet............................Mr. Wolff

Act II.

1. Overture.. Pleyel
2. Song..Mr. Wolff
3. Duetto Violin and Violoncello......................Beval
   By Mr. Duport and an Amateur
4. Trio on the Grand Piano Forte, by..............Mr. Moller
5. Quartet Violin............................... Mr. Reinagle
6. Finale... [195]

THIRD CONCERT, FEB. 19.

Act I.

1. Grand Overture of...............................Hayden
2. Sonato Piano Forte..........................Miss Moller
3. Quartett Violin...................................Pleyel
4. Concerto Clarinet...........................Mr. Wolff
5. Solo Violin (in which are introduced some favorite Scotch airs)
   Mr. Reinagle

Act II.

1. Overture....................................... Stamitz
2. Concerto Violoncello, by an Amateur.
3. Sonato Piano Forte..........................Mr. Moller
4. A favorite Concerto of La Motte by Master Duport
5. Finale... [196]

FOURTH CONCERT, MAR. 5.

Act. I.

1. Grand Overture of...............................Hayden
2. Miscellaneous Quartet...................... Mr. Reinagle

---

[195] *Am. Daily Adv.*, Feb. 1, 1791.
[196] *Am. Daily Adv.*, Feb. 16, 1791.

3. Sonato, Grand Piano Forte......................Mr. Moller
4. Quartetto, Clarinet...........................Mr. Wolff
5. Concerto, Grand Piano........................Miss Moller
6. Quartet, Violin....................................Pleyel
7. Finale.

Act. II.

1. Overture of..Hayden
 After the Concert Master Duport will perform a Grand Dance."[197]

FIFTH CONCERT, MAR. 26.
Act I.

1. Grand Overture of...............................Hayden
2. Song.
3. Sonato, Piano Forte...........................Miss Moller
4. Quartete, Clarinet..................................Wolff
5. Overture

Act II.

1. Overture of.......................................Gossec
2. Song.
3. Miscellaneous Quartett..........................Reniagle
4. Concerto Piano Forte..............................Moller
5. Finale.[198]

SIXTH CONCERT, APR. 16.
Act I.

1. Overture... Ditters
2. Sonata Grand Pianoforte......................Miss Moller
3. Song...Mrs. Gee
4. Concerto, Clarinetto...........................Mr. Wolff
5. Overture..Abel

---

[197]*Am. Daily Adv.*, Mar. 4, 1791.
[198]*Am. Daily Adv.*, Mar. 23, 1791.

ACT II.

1. Overture...Ld. Kelly
2. Song..Mrs. Gee
3. Quartett Violin...............................Mr. Reniagle
4. Concerto Grand Piano Forte.....................Mr. Moller
5. Finale of.......................................Haydn[199]

LAST CONCERT OF THE SEASON, APR. 30.

ACT I.

1. Overture...Abel
2. Sonata Piano Forte...........................Miss Moller
3. Song..Mrs. Gee
4. Concerto Clarinetto............................Mr. Wolff

ACT II.

1. Overture.. Stamitz
2. Song..Mrs Gee
3. Miscellaneous Quartett........................Mr. Reinagle
4. Concerto Piano Forte.........................Miss Moller
5. Finale of.......................................Haydn[200]

Besides the City Concerts, so-called Amateur Concerts were given at an early period and were still kept up in 1791, contrary to the belief of O. G. Sonneck. For instance there are advertisements and programs showing that the usual standard of concert-music was performed

"AMATEURS' CONCERT.

A concert will be performed at Mr. Henry Epple's, at Seven o'clock this Evening."[201]

Again we are notified that "this Evening the 3d instant there will be a Ball, only."[202] It seems probable that these concerts were followed by a dance.

---

[199]*Am. Daily Adv.*, April 13, 1791.
[200]*Am. Daily Adv.*, Apr. 29, 1791.
[201]*Am. Daily Adv.*, Feb. 3, 1791.
[202]*Am. Daily Adv.*, Mar. 3, 1791.

Also benefit concerts were still given as the following shows:

Benefit Concert for Master Duport, Mar. 19.

Act I.

1. Overture of...Abel
2. Concerto, Violin...........................Master Duport
3. Quartett Clarinet......................................Wolff
4. Sonato, Piano Forte.........................Reinagle
5. Overture...Hayden

Act II.

1. Overture ....Vanhal
2. Trio of...Boccherini
3. Overture, "La Divan de Village" of............Rousseau[203]

Benefit Concert for Miss Moller, Apr. 2.

Act I.

1. Overture...Ditters
2. Song...Mrs. Gee
3. Sonato, Grand Piano Forte.....................Miss Moller
4. Concerto, Clarinetto...........................Mr. Wolff
5. Duetto, Violoncello and Grand Piano Forte, by an Amateur and Mr. Moller.
6. Finale...Haydn

Act II.

1. Grand Overture.................................. Martini
2. Song...Mrs. Gee
3. Quartetto......................Messrs. Reinagle, etc., etc.
4. Duetto, Grand Piano Forte.....................Miss Moller
5. Finale ....Martini[204]

Concerts were given, too, at Vauxhall with programs equally as good as those of the City and Amateur Concerts, and an orchestra was undoubtedly present.[205]

[203]*Am. Daily Adv.*, Mar. 17, 1791.
[204]*Am. Daily Adv.*, Apr. 2, 1791.
[205]*Am. Daily Adv.*, Aug. 30, 1791.

"Vocal and Instrumental Concert at Vauxhall, May 18.

FIRST ACT.

1. A Grand Overture of.................................Haydn
2. Sinfonia ....Stamitz
3. Solo Rondo Violin................................Phile
4. Quartetto Violin.................................Davaux
5. Sinfonia...Vanhall

SECOND ACT.

1. Sinfonia of......................................Abel
2. Song—Bright Phoebus.
3. Quartetto Violino...............................Kammell
4. Fisher's Rondo, Clarinett by....................Mr. Wolff
5. Sinfonia...Abel
   After which Harmony, Music and Songs."[206]

VAUXHALL CONCERT, MAY 27.

FIRST ACT.

1. Overture of.....................................Lachmits
2. Sinfonia..Stamitz
3. Quartetto Violin................................Davaux
4. Song, by..Mrs. Kenna
5. Sinfonia..Abel

SECOND ACT

1. Overture..Phile
2. Quartetto, Clarinetto...........................Wolff
3. A Duetto, Song by...................Mr. and Mrs. Kenna
4. Quartetto.......................................Schultz
5. Sinfonia ....Kammel
   Harmony Music and Songs by Mr. and Mrs. Kenna.[207]

---

[206]*Am. Daily Adv.*, May 17, 1791.
[207]*Am. Daily Adv.*, May 25, 1791.

VAUXHALL CONCERT, SEPT. 2.

1. Grand Overture of............................Martini
2. Ditto.. Hayden
3. Ditto......................................Selime and Azor
4. Concerto, Violin by..............................Mr. Phile
5. Solo Rondo, Clarinet, by.......................Mr. Wolff
3. Ditto......................................Selime and Azor
4. Concerto, Violin............................by Mr. Phile
5. Solo Rondo, Clarinet,......................by Mr. Wolff
6. Song, by....................................Mr. Wolff[208]

By comparing these programs it will be readily seen that the performers in the City Concerts also take part in the Amateur and Vauxhall Concerts, etc., so we may be sure that the concerts were all about on a par.

———————

The City Concerts were continued the next season.[209] The following announcement was made concerning them:

"City Concert,
Of Vocal and Instrumental Music.
Under the direction of Messrs. Reinagle and Moller. The vocal parts by Mrs. Sewel and Mrs. Morris. The concert will commence on Saturday the 19th instant, at the Assembly Room, in Chestnut street."[210]

FIRST CONCERT, NOV. 19.

Act I.

1. New Overture of.............................Mr. Moller
2. Hunting song ....Mrs. Morris
3. Concerto, grand piano forte....................Miss Moller
4. Quartetto, violin........................Mr. Reinagle, etc.
5. Overture.

———————

[208]*Am. Daily Adv.*, Sept. 2, 1791.
[209]Sonneck, *Early Concert Life*, p. 87.
[210]*Am. Daily Adv.*, Nov. 9, 1791.

Act II.

1. Overture of..Pichl
2. Duett, violin and viola of........................Stamitz
3. Song..Mrs. Morris
4. Sonato, piano forte and violin,..........Moller and Reinagle[211]

SECOND CONCERT, DEC. 3.

Act I.

1. Overture of...Abel
2. Song...Mrs. Morris
3. Sonata, Pianoforte ....Miss Moller
4. Miscellaneous Quartett...................Mr. Reinagle, etc.

Act II.

1. Overture...................................... Reinagle
2. Duetto, violin and viola.
3. Song..Mrs. Morris
4. Sonata, piano forte and violin............Moller and Reinagle
5. Finale of..Abel[212]

THIRD CONCERT, DEC. 17.

Act I.

1. Overture of..................................Stamitz, senr.
2. Duet,.....................Mrs. Morris and Mr. Reinagle
3. Sonata, Piano forte...........................Miss Moller
4. Quartett of...Pleyel
5. Overture...Abel

Act II.

1. Overture..Pichl
2. New Miscellaneous Quartett...................Mr. Reinagle
3. Song..Mrs. Morris
4. Sonata, Piano Forte.................Mr. Moller, of Pleyel
5. Finale... Abel[213]

---

[211]*Am. Daily Adv.*, Nov. 19, 1791.
[212]*Am. Daily Adv.*, Dec. 1, 1791.
[213]*Am. Daily Adv.*, Dec. 15, 1791.

FOURTH CONCERT, DEC. 31.

ACT I.

1. Overture, 4th Opera, 10 of...........................Abel
2. Song...Mrs. Morris
3. Sonata, Piano Forte...........................Miss Moller
4. Quartett of.......................................Pleyel
5. Periodical Overture................................Bach

ACT II.

1. Overture...Reinagle
2. Miscellaneous Quartett..........................Stamitz
3. Song...Mrs. Morris
4. Concerto, Piano Forte, ...Mr. Mollen, of Schroeter
5. Finale...................................... Abel[214]

FIFTH CONCERT, JAN 14, 1792

ACT I.

1. Overture of.......................................Moller
2. Song (from the New opera of the Woodman)........Mrs. Morris
3. Sonata, Piano Forte...........................Miss Moller
4. Concerto, French horn....................Mons. Pelissier
5. Periodical Overture of...............................Abel

ACT II.

1. Overture of.................................. Holtzwara
2. The ist Miscellaneous Quartett of...................Vachon
3. Song (Damon's all inconstancy)..................Mrs. Morris
4. Concerto, Piano Forte........................Mr. Moller
5. Finale.................................... [215]

SIXTH CONCERT

ACT I.

1. Overture 44th of...............................Vanhall
2. Hunting Song...............................Mrs. Morris

---

[214]*Am. Daily Adv.*, Dec. 30, 1791.
[215]*Am. Daily Adv.*, Jan. 12, 1792.
[216]*Am. Daily Adv.*, Jan. 28, 1792.

3. Sonata Piano Forte...........................Miss Moller
4. Miscellaneous Quartett.......................Mr. Reinagle

Act II.

1. Overture to Rosina................................Shield
2. Song (from the Woodman).....................Mrs. Morris
3. Concerto, Piano Forte........................Mr. Moller
4. Quartett, French Horn........................Mr. Pellisier
5. Overture of.....................................Jomelli[216]

SEVENTH CONCERT, FEB. 11.

Act I.

1. Overture Ist of.............................M. A. Guenin
2. Song...Mrs. Morris
3. Sonata, Piano Forte..........................Miss Moller
4. Quartett of Pleyel......................Mr. Reinagle, etc.
5. Overture 2d................................M. A. Guenin

Act II.

1. Overture of......................................Stamitz
2. Duetto, Violin and Viola.................Moller and Reinagle
3. Song...Mrs. Morris
4. Concerto, Piano Forte........................Mr. Moller
5. Finale.. Abel[217]

EIGHTH AND LAST CITY CONCERT OF THE SEASON HELD MAR. 10.

Act I.

1. Overture 6th, op. 10, of.............................Abel
2. Song...Mrs. Morris
3. Sonata, Piano Forte..........................Miss Moller
4. Quartett, Pleyel........................ Mr. Reinagle, etc.
5. Overture...Haydn

---

[217]*Am. Daily Adv.*, Feb. 11, 1792.

Act II.
1. Overture 57.....................................Vanhall
2. Miscellaneous Quartett
3. Song...Mrs. Morris
4. Concerto Piano Forte.........................Mr. Moller
5. Finale.. Crispi[218]

Finally a "City Concert Benefit" was given for Miss Moller.

Act I.
1. Overture, by......................................Pichl
2. Song, The Traveller benighted, ...Miss Moller
3. Quartette, French Horn.......................Mr. Pellisier
4. Grand Ariette, Sorti, with accompaniment by a Guitar, composed by............... ....Mr. Cassaignard, Amateur
5. Concerto Violin...............................Mr. Phile

Act II.
1. Overture by...Abel
2. Ariette Du Marquis de Floriant, by...Mr. Cassaignard, Amateur
3. Concerto Piano Forte.........................Miss Moller
4. Duetto, Violin and Tenor..........Messrs Reinagle and Moller
5. Finale.......................................Vanhall [219]

Foot-Note; At a concert given at Vauxhall in 1792 the instrumental parts were taken by a number of Germans: Messrs. Phile, Schulz, Tremner, [*Scotchman Bremner*,] Roth, Christhilf, Spangenberg etc., (Cf. *Am. Daily Adv.* June 8, 1792).
Cf. Durang, *History of the Stage in Phila.*, Chapter 12, who gives the name Trimmer.

A glance at these programs or at the City Concert programs published by Sonneck[220] should convince anyone that the musical taste of Philadelphia was good, also that the German composers were favorites—at least with the managers—and a predilection was shown for Abel, Stamitz, Pleyel, and Haydn."

[218]*Am. Daily Adv.*, Mar. 8, 1792.
[219]*Am. Daily Adv.*, Mar. 31, 1792.
[220]For a full discussion of concert life Cf. Sonneck, (*Early Concert Life*), as well for French, English, and German influence.

Reinagle was not only interested in the artistic production of music, but also, according to one writer, in the industrial development. He is said to have had a share in the piano manufactory established by Charles Tawes.[221]

Concerning the residence of Reinagle in Philadelphia, his contemporaries have something to say. At that time Wignell was an important factor in the theatrical world and in the fall of 1791 he "associated himself with Mr. Reinagle, a professor of music in Philadelphia, and a composer of some note at that time.[222] They founded the first Chestnut Street Theatre, "the corner stone of which was laid by Mr. Reinagle, a Master Mason, in Masonic form."[223]

The new theatre was opened to the public for the first time on Saturday evening, April 2d, 1793, "with a grand concert of vocal and instrumental music."[224]

"The orchestra department was under the direction of Manager Reinagle, and the musicians were deemed equal in ability with the stage artists. In truth the orchestra contained about twenty accomplished musicians, many of them of great notoriety as concerto players on their respective instruments.

"The concentration of that early date of so much dramatic, operatic and instrumental talent, introduced a new era of theatricals here.

"Who that once saw old manager Reinagle in his official capacity, could ever forget his dignified personne. He presided at his piano forte, looking the very personification of the patriarch of music—investing the science of harmonious sounds, as well as the dramatic school, with a moral influence, reflecting and adorning its salutary uses with high respectability and polished manners. His appearance was of the reverent and impressive kind, which at once inspired the universal respect of the audience. Such was Reinagle's imposing appearance, that it awed the disorderly of the

---

[221]Cf. D. Spillane, *History of the Am. Pianoforte,* p. 99.
[222]Durang, *History of the Stage in Philadelphia,* chapter 15.
[223]Durang, *History of the Stage in Philadelphia,* chapter 19.
[224]Durang, *History of Stage in Philadelphia,* chapter 19.

galleries, or the fop of annoying propensities, and impertinent criticism of the box lobby into decorum.

"It was inspiring to behold the polished Reinagle saluting from his seat (before the grand square piano forte in the orchestra) the highest respectability of the city, as it entered the boxes to take seats. It was a scene before the curtain that suggested a picture of the master of private ceremonies receiving his invited guests at the fashionable drawing room.

"Mr. Reinagle was a gentleman and a musician. His compositions evinced decided cleverness and originality, and some of his accompaniments to the old opera music were much admired by good judges."[225]

An article by William McKoy presents a clearer picture of Mr. Reinagle. He says:

"Mr. Reinagle, one of the Managers, and a Professor of Music, used to be seen, but only on particular occasions, seated at the Piano Forte, then standing against the stage, in the rear of the band [orchestra] for the mere purpose of touching a few notes solo, by way of accompaniment to the silvery tones of Mrs. Wignell. * * * Mr. Reinagle, while thus enjoying the effect of her inimitable chant, exhibited to the audience a head not unlike that of Louis the XIV but divested of the simplicity, bushy, powdered hair, large high forehead, and round full face, illuminated by silver mounted spectacle glasses, a perceptible smirk at all times about the mouth, and an extraordinary depth of dimple in his cheek, while sitting there and surveying the irritability of Mr. Gillingham, the Leader of the Band, on his being obliged to leave the music of Handel and Mozart, and strike off into the 'President's March.' "[226]

In Durang's account, the compositions of Reinagle are spoken of highly; there is the testimony of another man, an actor in Reinagle's company, to substantiate the above eulogy, as follows (1804):

"By the death of Wignell * * * the management devolved upon his widow and Reinagle. * * * The musical

[225]Durang, chapter 19.
[226]Poulson's *Daily Advertiser*, January 13, 1829.

department fell of course to the charge of Reinagle, whose compositions and adaptations were deserved favorites with the public."[227]

Again, there is the testimony of a man of our own times to show that the above praise was not undeserved. Speaking of some of Reinagle's sonatas, O. G. Sonneck says:

"These sonatas follow closely in the footsteps of Ph. Em. Bach and the early Haydn without being void of individuality. If the larger works of Reinagle all were as fine and effective as these sonatas he must have been a composer of merit."[228]

Sonneck has published titles of forty-two works ascribed to Reinagle,[229] to which we have added several others some of which are still in existence. These compositions include sonatas, overtures, preludes, songs, opera music, adaptations, accompaniments, etc.

From all this evidence it will appear that Alexander Reinagle must have been a great force in music in Philadelphia, and did much to shape the taste of the people for good music—especially for German music, and may thus be called the greatest German American musician of that century.

Concerning his home life, it is known that Reinagle was married and had two sons, Hugh, a scenic painter of some note, and Thomas. The later years of his life Reinagle spent in the management of a theatre in Baltimore, where he died September 21, 1809.[230]

---

[227]Wood, Personal *Recollections of the Stage*, p. 104.

[228]Sonneck, *Early Secular American Music*, p. 13.

[229]Cf. Sonneck, *Early Secular American Music*, p. 139.

[230]Durang, chapters 19 and 24.

Note: For a list of Reinagle's compositions, Cf. **Appendix**.

CHAPTER VIII.

Philip Roth and Philip Phile

Although Alexander Reinagle was the greatest musician of this period there were others of importance as Juhan, Moller, Capron, Brown, Schetky, Wolff, etc., etc. It is not our intention to take up these men separately, as material is too scanty to warrant it. Sonneck has given short biographies of most of these men.[231] There are two men, however, Philip Phile and Philip Roth about whom we know considerable. They were both musicians of no mean calibre, appeared frequently in the concerts given in Philadelphia, and were also composers of music.

Philip Roth's first public appearance, as far as is known, was in 1771 at the benefit concert of John M'Lean, when an overture composed by him "for the occasion" was performed.[232] This piece was, perhaps, the first of importance composed by a German in Philadelphia. The advertisement speaks of him as "Master of the Band, belonging to his Majesty's Royal Regiment of North British Fusileers." However, as will be shown later, he was undoubtedly a true German.

From 1771 to 1785 we lose sight of Roth, but then he appears as a music teacher in Philadelphia.[233] It is quite likely that he was here still earlier. He lived in Philadelphia from 1785 on until his death in 1804.

The importance of Philip Roth lies in the fact that it has been claimed by some, that he is the composer of "The President's March" to which the song "Hail Columbia" was set. Others claim that Philip Phile was the author. The claims of Philip Roth, which at

---

[231]Sonneck, *Early Secular American Music*, Index.
[232]See Above, p. 54.
[233]Cf. *City Directory of Philadelphia*, 1785.

the most are meagre, rest upon an article in a newspaper of 1829, written by Wm. McKoy, twenty-five years after Roth was dead. This article, as will be shown, contains one error, and may contain others. The article in question reads thus:

"The seat of the Federal Government of the thirteen United States being removed to Philadelphia, and in honor of the new President Washington, then residing at No. 190 High Street, the March, ever since known as the President's March, was composed by a German Teacher of Music, in this city, named Roth, or Roat, designated familiarly by those who knew him, as 'Old Roat.' He taught those of his pupils who preferred the flute, to give to that instrument the additional sound of the drone, while playing in imitation of the Scotch Bagpipe. His residence was at one time in that row of houses back from Fifth, above Race street, at that time known as "The Fourteen Chimnies' some of which [1829] are still visible in the rear ground, north eastward of Mayer's Church. In his person he was of the middle size and height. His face was truly German in expression; dark gray eyes, and bushy eye-brows, round pointed nose, prominent lips, and parted chin. He took snuff immoderately, having his ruffles and vest usually sprinkled with grains of rappee. He was considered an eccentric and a kind of drole. He was well known *traditionally* at the Sampson and Lion, in Crown Street, where it seems, his company, in the Olden Time was always a welcome addition to the Pewter Pint Customers, gathered there, at their Pipes and Beer, while listening to his facetious tales and anecdotes, without number, of High Life about Town, and of the Players: Nick Hammond, Miss Tuke, Hodgkinson, Mrs. Pownall, and Jack Martin of the Old Theatre in Southwark. This said President's March, by Roat, the popular songs of Markoe,[234] the City Poet, in particular the one called 'The Taylor done over,' and the beautiful air of 'Dans Votre Lit,' . . . . . were sung and whistled by everyone who felt freedom (of mind) to whistle and sing.

* * *

"Public opinion having . . . . released itself from a passion for French Revolutionary Musick and Song, experienced a vacuum in that particular, which was immediately supplied by the new, National American Song of 'Hail Columbia happy Land,' written in

---

[234]Peter Markoe (1768-1792) born at Santa Cruz, West Indies, educated in Eng., died at Phila.

'98, by Joseph Hopkinson, Esq.[235] of this city, and the measure adapted by him very judiciously, to the almost forgotten President's March. Even since 1798, the song of Hail Columbia, by Joseph Hopkinson, and the President's March, by *Johannes* Roat, being indiscriminately called for, have become, in a manner synonymous to the public ear and understanding, when they are actually and totally distinct in their origin, as above mentioned.

"Such was the popularity of the song, that very frequently has Mr. Gillingham, Leader of the Band, [Orchestra], been forced to come to a full stop in the *foreign* music, he had arranged for the evening by the deafening calls for this march, or song to the march."[236]

In the first place, we wish to pick out a few errors, which will show why we must use this testimony with caution. The writer says that Roth was "well known traditionally," evidently not personally known to him. Again he says that the "President's March" at the time "Hail Columbia" was written was "almost forgotten," but on the contrary the actor, Gilbert Fox, urged Joseph Hopkinson to set words to that tune on account of its popularity. Thirdly, he says that the march was written by *Johannes* Roat. This is evidently an error in the Christian name due to traditions as we will try to show. We have gone carefully through the city directories from 1785 (when they were first printed,) to 1806; also the newspapers of that time, and wills and letters of administration but find no record of a "Johannes" Roat. We find a *Philip* Roth, and we shall strive now to give proof that they were one and the same, as so far there has been no adequate statement of this fact.

To recapitulate: Philip Roth, we have already discovered, was a Band Master in a British regiment in Philadelphia, and wrote an overture in 1771.[237] All trace of him is lost during the war, but he probably continued to fill his position in the British Army, or possibly the same position in the U. S. army.

---

[235]Son of Francis Hopkinson mentioned above as an important figure in Phila. musical development, Cf. Above, pp. ff.

[236]Poulson's *Daily Advertiser*, Jan. 13, 1829.

[237]Cf. Above, p. 54.

[238]*Pa. Jour.*, Sept. 10, 1788.

In 1785 there is the name Philip Roots in the city directory. In 1788 he has an advertisement in the newspaper,[238] while in 1789 we have the following:

"Mr. Roth, Music Master, In Pennington Alley running from Race to Vine Streets, between Fourth and Fifth Streets.

"Teaches all kinds of Instrumental Music in the shortest manner, viz. Harpsichord or Piano Forte, Guitar, Flute, Hautboy, Clarinet, Bassoon, French Horn, Harp and Thorough-Bass, which is the Ground of Music, etc."[239]

In this advertisement we have Mr. Roth; not Philip nor Johannes. This would imply that the above-mentioned man was the only person in Philadelphia by the name of Roth who was a music teacher. There was no city directory after 1785 until 1791. In this year there appears this entry:

"Philip Roth, musician 25 Crown St."[240]

Now turning to the advertisement again we read that Mr. Roth lived:

"In Pennington Alley running from Race to Vine Streets, between Fourth and Fifth streets." But the city directory informs us that Crown St., and Pennington Alley were one and the same.[241] To go a step further, let us compare the article on the 'President's March,' above quoted, as to the abode of Johannes Roat, which says:

"His residence was at *one* time in that row of houses back from Fifth, above Race street, at that time known as 'The Fourteen Chimneys' . . . . north-eastward from Mayer's Church."[242]

Now comparing these three dwelling places, we find that they were on the same street—at least two of them—and the third in the same neighborhood; but we find that there was only one man, which our evidence gives, so we may be perfectly sure that the other two men may be fused into the one—Philip Roth. This man lived, while he was in Philadelphia in one locality as the directories show.

---

[239]*Pa. Jour.*, Jan. 7, 1789.
[240]*City Directory*, 1791, p. 110.
[241]*City Directory*, 1795, p. 81.
[242]Cf. Above p. 77.

1791   Philip Roth, musician, 25 Crown St.
1795 Philip Roth, 31 Race St.
1798   Philip Roth, Crown St.
1797   Philip Roth musician, Crown St.
1798   Philip Roth, musician Crown St.
1799   Philip Roth, teacher of music, 33 Crown St.
1800   Philip Roth, teacher of music, 33 Crown St.
1801   Philip Roth, music master, 33 Crown St.
1802   Philip Roth, music master, 33 Crown St.
1803   Philip *Rote*, music master, 33 Crown St.
1804   Philip *Rote*, music master, 33 Crown St.

His name is also given in the directory of 1805, but nevertheless he died in 1804.

From the above, it is seen that he lived on the same street all the time he was in Philadelphia, with the exception of the year 1795 when he dwelt at 31 Race St., which however, was not far away. We see, too, the different appellations given to him, as "musician," "teacher of music," and finally "master of music," Evidently he was skilled as a musician, and was respected as such.

Little else is known about Philip Roth, but we may presume that he played in the orchestra of the "Old Southwark Theatre"— perhaps was even the leader, since we know that he was well acquainted with the actors.[243]   We do know that he composed a piece of music, or rather set to music a "Hunting Song," which was printed in the "Universal Asylum," April, 1790.   He must indeed, have been a skilful musician to be able to give lessons on all the instruments in his advertisement—nine in all—although he could not have been proficient on all.   Still he must have been talented.

The date of his death has been misstated by the only author, who has mentioned it at all.   O. G. Sonneck, in his book *"Early Secular American Music"* (1905) page 190, and in an article *"Critical Notes on the Origin of Hail Columbia"* printed in the *"Sammelbaende der Internationalen Musik-Gesellschaft"* (1901) states that Philp Roth died in 1805.

---

[243]Cf. Above, p. 89.

It is true that in the City Directory for 1805 his name is found while in the directory for 1806 the following entry appears:

"Rote, widow of Philip, music master, 94 N. 7th St."[144]

To offset the above evidence there is the documentary proof as follows:

"On the 24th day of September, 1804, Letters of Administration were granted unto Mary Roth on the Estate of her Husband, Philip Roth deceased.

$200.   Henry Lies of Philadelphia, Victualler.   Jacob Grace of Nor. Liberties,   Carter.   Sureties."[245]

Philip Roth could not have amassed much wealth during his musical career, since his surety was only $200.

So much for Philip Roth and his claims as author of the "Presidents March." The other claimant is Philip Phile, about whom we know as little as about Philip Roth.   As early as 1784 Phile was in Philadelphia; as there is a concert advertised for his benefit in that year.[246]   Somewhat later than this Durang, a contemporary of Phile tells us that:

"The orchestra at the beginning of the "Old American Company" production was Mr. Philo, *leader*; Mr. Bentley, harpsichord; Mr. Woolf, principal clarinet, Trimmer, Hecker, and son, violoncello, violins, etc.   Some six or seven other names, now not remembered, constituted the musical force.   The *latter* were *all* Germans."[247]

Mr. Phile was occupying a somewhat important position—the leadership of a *German* orchestra numbering some twelve or thirteen men.   From now on until his death in 1793,[248] Phile wandered back and forth between New York and Philadelphia.   In 1784 he appears on the concert programs in the latter city.   In 1786 with Alexander Reinagle he played a duet for violin and 'cello in New York,[249]

---

[244]*City Directory*, 1806.
[245]Cf. *Letters of Administration, Book K*, No. 156, p. 178 in office of Recorder of Wills, City Hall, Philadelphia.
[246]*Pa. Packet*, Mar. 6, 1784.
[247]Durang, *History of the Stage in Phila.*, Chapter 12, [A rare book].
[248]Sonneck, *Early Secular American Music*, p. 189.
[249]*N. Y. Packet*, Jul. 13, 1786.

while the next year he is back again in Philadelphia.[250]   In 1792 he takes part in a concert together with Philip Roth and other Germans.[251]   Perhaps Roth was a member of his orchestra.   After 1789 he apparently settled down in Philadelphia, and lived on Race St., between Front and Second.[252]

Such is the knowledge we have concerning Phile's life.   Let us consider what are his claims to the authorship of the "President's March."   As in the case of Roth, the march was claimed for Phile by his friends; but in his case there are two different accounts of its origin as follows: 1.   First it was claimed for him by his son, who says he was present when it was played.   He says that the march was composed by his father, and played at Trenton Bridge in 1789 in honor of Washington, who was on his way to New York to be inaugurated.[253]   2.   Second, it is said by the nephew of Washington, G. W. Custis (1860), that this march was played in the John St. Theatre, N. Y., Nov. 24, 1789 in honor of Washington, who was present that evening.   The composer is said to be a German named Feyles.[254]   "Feyles" is a corruption of Phile and we also find it spelled Philo, Phylo, Phyla, Phyle, Phyles, Fyles, etc.

There are, then, two different statements as to the composition of this piece by Phile, which would lead us to think, that, in the minds of the people it was a doubtful question as to how and when this march was composed.   To add to this, the claim that Philip Roth composed this march, only makes the situation more confused. Sonneck has pointed out in his article *"Critical Notes on the Origin of Hail Columbia,"*[255] that there was no account in the daily papers of that time concerning this march, as there probably would have been, had it been composed in honor of so important a man as Washington.   He, however, inclines to the belief that Phile did write

[250]*Pa. Packet*, Jan. 13, 1787.

[251]See Above, Note to 72.

[252]Sonneck, *Article* in Sammelbände (1901), p. 156.

[253]*Baltimore Clipper*, 1841.

[254]G. W. Custis, *Recollections and Private Memoirs of Washing.* p. 368.
Also *Diary of Geo. Wash.* 1789-1791, (ed. B. J. Lossing, 1860), p. 56.

[255]*Sammelbaender Internationalen Musik Gesellschaft*, 1901.

the march; but until a manuscript with the name of the composer thereon is discovered, we cannot say with surety who did write it.[256] We have, then, these two composers before us and can pay our money and take our choice.

Concerning the compositions of these two men we know little. The overture composed by Roth in 1771 has already been mentioned. Sonneck also gives a "Hunting Song" set to music by Mr. Roth in 1790. Sonneck credits Phile with the following compositions.

1787

1. Violin Concerto by Mr. Phile.

1790

2. Harmony Music, Phile.[257]

In addition to these we have:

1791

3. Overture by P. to be played at Vauxhall Concert, May 27.[258]
4. Concerto Violin by Mr. Phile. At Vauxhall Sept. 2.[259]

---

[256]Many writers have expressed an opinion, but evidently their information consisted of a knowledge of only *one claim*.

[257]Cf. Sonneck, *Early Sec. Am. Music* for these compositions.

[258]*Am. Daily Adv.*, May 25, 1791.

[259]*Am. Daily Adv.*, Sept. 2, 1791.

CONCLUSION.

We have tried to show the gradual growth of musical taste in Philadelphia, especially the taste for German music. As before mentioned this taste was undoubtedly stimulated mostly by the English musicians, at least until the last period. In that period the English, and German musicians, seem to have worked in conjunction to keep up the standard set by their predecessors. It must not be thought that German music alone ruled in Philadelphia. During the French Revolution, especially, many refugees arrived in Philadelphia and concerts of French music were given and great enthusiasm was aroused among the American citizens. However, on looking over the whole century, German music seems to predominate over the music of other nations in Philadelphia. Musical taste in Philadelphia after the Revolution will compare favorably with the taste shown in Europe at the same period.

APPENDIX.

WORKS OF ALEXANDER REINAGLE.

Unless otherwise noted this list has been taken from O. G. Sonneck's *"Early Secular American Music."* They are given here according to date of production.

1787.

1. Overture.
2. "A Select Collection of the most favorite Scots tunes. With variations for the pianoforte or harpsichord."
3. A song (newly composed).

1788.

4. *"Federal March,* as performed in the grand procession in Philadelphia, the 4th of July, 1788. Composed and adapted for the pianoforte, violin, or German flute."

1789.

5. Song.
"Adieu thou dreary pile."
Arranged for pianoforte or harpsichord by Reinagle.
6. *Chorus,* sung before Gen. Washington, as he passed under the triumphal arch on Trenton Bridge, April 21, 1789. "Set to music and dedicated by permission to Mrs. Washington."
7. *Song.* "In vain fond youth you would conceal."
8. *Song.* "My soul is thine, sweet Nora."
9. *Song.* "The Soldier tried, etc."
10. *Song.* "Tantive back forward."
11. *Song.* "Tis not the bloom on Damon's cheek."
(These songs were *arranged* by R. for pianoforte or harpsichord.)
12. Overture. "La Schiava" (Piccini.)
13. Overture to opera "Maria" (Shield).
(These overtures arranged for pf. by R.)

1791.

14.   Song. "Winter." Set to music by R. with pf. acc.

15.   Miscellaneous Quartet. Played at the "City Concert" Mar. 5, 1791 and often the remainder of the season.[260]   This composition is dated by Sonneck 1793.

16.   *New* Miscellaneous Quartet. To be played at the "City Concert" Dec. 17, 1791.[261]

1794.

17.   Song. "America, Commerce and Freedom." By. R.

18.   "La Chasse" (Rosetti). Arranged for pianoforte or Harpsichord by R.

19.   *"Concerto* On the Improved Pianoforte with Additional keys.

20.   "La Foret Noire (serious pantomime. *Overture,* etc., entirely new, composed by Mr. Reinagle.")

21.   Occasional Overture.

22.   *"Preludes* in three classes, for the improvement of practitioners on the pianoforte."

23.   "Robin Hood" (comic opera,) original overture by Baumgarten, additional airs by R.

24.   "Slaves in Algiers" (play interspersed with songs), Music by R.

24.   "Spanish Barber" (opera translated from Beaumarchais, by G. Colemann), additional airs by Reinagle and Carr.

1795.

26.   "Harlequin shipwreck'd" (Pantomime).   New music by R.

27.   "Harlequins invasion" (Pantomime.)   New medley overture by R.

28.   "Volunteers" (comic opera). Music and overture entirely new.

29.   "The Purse" (musical drama by J. J. Cross), accompaniments and new airs by R.

---

[260]Cf. *Am. Daily Adv.*, Mar. 4, 1791.   Also programs given in this book for 1791.

[261]Cf. *Am. Daily Adv.*, Dec. 15, 1791.

30. "Auld Robin Gray" (opera), new music and a Scottish medley overture by R.

1796.

31. "Mountaineers" (comic opera), accompaniments by R.
32. "Pierre de Province and La Belle Magulone" new music by R. This was also called "The Rival Knights" or La "Belle Magalone" a pantomime.[262] Probably this was the same thing as "Pierre de Province "although the latter was advertised as a "ballet."
33. "Grand Divertisement in the Temple of Liberty taken from the celebrated Ballet, called, Warriors Welcome Home. The Overture and Music compiled by Mr. Reinagle in which is introduced a number of Irish and Scotch Airs."[263]
34. "The Shamrock" (Irish dance), Irish medley Overture by R.[264]
35. "Witches of the rocks or Harlequin everywhere" (Pantomime), "with an entire new overture, songs, choruses, and recitations composed by Mr. Reinagle."

1797.

36. "Columbus" (historical play), incidental music by R.
37. Savoyard (musical farce), music by R.

1798.

38. " 'The Gentle Shepherd', written by Allan Ramsay. With original airs and the accompaniment by Mr. Reinagle." This was called "the favorite comical Scot's Pastoral" and was to be performed at the New Theatre.[265]
39. "Italian Monk" (opera), music and accompaniment by R.

1799.

40. Monody. "On the Death of the much lamented, the late Lieutenant-General of the Armies of the United States. The

---

[262]Cf. *Am. Daily Adv.*, Jun. 27, 1796.
[263]Cf. *Am. Daily Adv.*, Mar. 28, 1796.
[264]Perhaps the same as advertised in *Am. Daily Adv.*, May. 7, 1794.
[265]*Am. Daily Adv.*, Apr. 16, 1798.

Music composed by R. Taylor, and Mr. Reinagle." To be given at the New Theatre.[266]

41. "Blue Beard" (opera accompaniments by R.)

42. The Arabs of the desert, or Harlequins flight from Egypt," with a new Overture and Music, composed by Mr. Reinagle."[267]

Probably before 1800 (date not known).

43. Collection of favorite songs, divided into books. The basses rendered easy and natural for the pianoforte or harpsichord by Alex. Reinagle."

1800.

44. Masonic overture.

45. "Naval pillar" (musical entertainment), accompaniments by R.

46. "Pizarro," by Kotzebue; adapted by R. B. Sheridan; music by Reinagle and Raynor Taylor.

---

[266]*Am. Daily Adv.*, Dec. 23, 1799.
[267]Cf. *Am. Daily Adv.*, Apr., 13, 1799.